Michael Prichard's
POCKET GUIDE
FRESHWATER FISHING

KT-433-457

50p

Michael Prichard started writing in the hard school of Fleet Street, and having acquired the skills of the journalist he left for quieter waters. As a fishing tackle adviser, he travels far and wide in the pursuit of good tackle design. He has directed a number of angling films, and broadcasts regularly on radio and TV.

With a life-long fascination with fishing in all its forms, Mike has sought every species of interest to the sportfisherman and succeeded in taking many fine specimens from freshwater and saltwater. His prowess with the camera (he is an Associate of the Royal Photographic Society) enables him to publish first-class evidence of his catches. In 1978 and 1979 Mike captained England at International Sea Fishing festivals in Connemara and Youghal, Eire, and in both years his team beat strong opposition from the rest of the British and Continental teams. For many years he also organized the popular Guinness sea angling contests in Dingle, Eire.

A desire to pass on his wide knowledge of the sport has led to the encouragement and instruction of young anglers in many areas of Britain. Among the author's books are his *Pocket Guide to Saltwater Fishing*, *Pocket Guide to Bait and Lures*, *Pocket Guide to Spinning* (the companions to this book), the best-selling *Encyclopedia of Fishing in Britain and Ireland*, and *Fishing for Beginners*, all published by Collins. He contributes regularly to both British and European angling magazines.

COMPANION BOOKS

Michael Prichard's Pocket Guide to Saltwater Fishing
Michael Prichard's Pocket Guide to Bait and Lures
Michael Prichard's Pocket Guide to Spinning

Michael Prichard's
POCKET GUIDE TO
FRESHWATER
FISHING

Collins

Published by William Collins Sons & Co. Ltd.
London and Glasgow.
Text, photographs and diagrams © Michael Prichard 1982
Fish profile paintings © William Collins Sons & Co. Ltd. 1977, 1982

First published 1982
Reprinted 1984

Printed and bound in Great Britain by
William Collins Sons & Co. Ltd.

ISBN 0 00 411645 3

CONTENTS

INTRODUCTION

Fishing is the most satisfying of all the sports undertaken in our countryside and around the shores of this land. Understandably, there are more followers for angling than any other sport or game. Anglers do not watch other people exerting themselves, they take part—and herein lies the magic of fishing.

Although I have caught many fish, some of great weight, some of exotic importance, I cannot truly explain just how I felt at the moment of capture. All I can hope to do within these pages is to set out the techniques and subtleties of the sport of fishing in freshwater, together with an explanation of the natural history of the species and a description of where they live. Then you, the angling reader, must follow your own path to successful fishing.

Basically, there are three forms of sportfishing: in freshwater for coarse fish species; in rivers, lakes and reservoirs for members of the salmon family; or, if you prefer being close to saltwater, for species that abound off the beaches, rocky shores and deep-water marks of our surrounding seas. (*Saltwater Fishing* is the title of the companion to this book.) Some anglers pursue more than one aspect of the sport, changing their mood and tackle as season or weather dictate, for there is always angling activity somewhere in these islands. Angling can be a reasonably simple country pursuit; success rarely depends on the amount of fishing tackle owned or the complexity of the rigs used. Of course there is a mechanical aspect to what we do and this many of us enjoy, even to the extent of proving ourselves masters of the art of casting, tackle and lure making, none of which demands a visit to the waterside! But it is in the understanding of our quarry and the environment in which they live that gives the greatest satisfaction—for are we not hunters? I have kept references concerning legislated close seasons to the minimum. Some countries do not have them—indeed there are parts of the United Kingdom where coarse fish do not enjoy a respite from anglers—but I believe in a close season for freshwater fish. Similarly, I feel that birds, animals and plantlife benefit from a period of rest and rejuvenation which can be assured by the absence of anglers during a few spring months.

In this volume I would like to introduce you to fishing in freshwater for coarse fish and the game species.

Michael Prichard, ARPS

The start of it all—the wonder of a small creature and the inevitable jam jar.

(Above) *A perfect fishery. Eire's Stones Lake contains specimen bream, tench in pollution-free conditions.* (Right) *Not all murky waters are polluted. Feeding bream root in the silt, creating turbid conditions in the Grand Canal, Co Kildare.* (Below) *Anglers curse the wind, but it replaces oxygen.* (Below right) *A healthy environment produces the best sportfishing.*

THE COARSE FISHING ENVIRONMENTS

Fish live in water and in order to achieve a healthy existence they require certain conditions. They need clean water, free from pollution that would cut down the amount of oxygen available for the fish to breathe. Water that contains man-made discharges of chemicals, drainage effluent or basic rubbish will also tend to be clouded, a condition that would prevent sunlight penetrating down through the depths to where plants grow. Lack of light ensures an underwater desert where plantlife cannot root and grow. The minute creatures that form the larger part of a fish's diet need plants on which to live, so a dirty stretch of water will normally mean a place devoid of life.

To the eye of the human being, some slow-running rivers or stillwaters may appear contaminated because they are muddy. But this is not a form of pollution at all. Probably the muddiness was caused by the activities of fish whose feeding behaviour, rooting around in the silt that forms the bed of the river or pool, stirs up mud for a period within the fish's day. Then the mud will settle, light will pierce the turbidity and the life cycle will continue.

A given volume of water is capable, subject to time of year and climatic condition, of carrying a particular amount of usable oxygen. During the winter the colder water contains vastly more oxygen. This oxygen is regularly replaced by heavy winter rainfall and from high winds that continuously ruffle the water surface. Greater amounts of water flow over weirs where the water falls from heights that force the intake of more of the life-giving gas. Unfortunately, in the warmer months of summer there is less rainfall, winds are generally softer and man makes a demand of our water resources by abstracting water from the rivers and streams. All these factors add up to a shortage of oxygen and a lack of dilution to the pollutants that find their way into the watercourses.

Nature provides signs, gives visible clues to clean water and a healthy fish habitat. Lush bankside vegetation and strong-growing waterweeds indicate clean water. The colour of the weed is another way in which to assess the quality of the water. Most water plants are a healthy green, never brownish-black with the telltale line of surface discoloration that hints of impurity.

Coarse fish are found in the slower-flowing rivers, streams and canals. They tolerate much lower levels of purity and oxygen content than the salmon family that are generally to be found in rocky rivers with steeper gradients giving faster flowing conditions.

Overgrown with lush waterweeds, the winding stream provides the essential cover that fish need for protection from their predators.

Small streams

All of our world's major rivers had to start somewhere so our classification of running water begins with the tiny stream. It may rise as a spring, from an underground catchment area or as the outlet from an area of bogland or marsh. When still very shallow, the small stream becomes capable of supporting life. The marshy ground will be a natural breeding ground for insects, such as mosquitos and midges. A large number of these creatures have a period in their life-cycle when they live under the water's surface. The larvae drift downstream where they become food for larger animals such as fish. Because the tiny rivulet normally begins life far from human habitation, and is often hidden away under lush grasses and sedges, it contains little pollution. Therefore it is a valuable larder for fish lower downstream.

Streams

Like the ribs on the reverse side of a leaf, tiny streams come together to form the stream where the sport of fishing really begins. A foot (30 cm) or so of water shrouded by over-hanging banks covered by plants and trees gives resident fish all of the conditions necessary to their lives: food that swims or drifts downstream, minute offerings that fall into the water from the over-hanging boughs, and security. These essential factors are brought about by the very nature of the winding path of the waterway and its surrounding tangles of undergrowth. Fish can grow and breed without the constant harassment of avian and human predation. Fish will grow large in the stream but as their numbers increase they tend to drop down toward the river where there is greater living space.

Rivers

There are many different types of river but they fall roughly into two angling categories: the smaller, steep-gradient river that drains highlands and which has a fast flow; and the wide, deep sluggish river that meanders through the flatlands. Both kinds of river provide good angling but of quite different natures. Each form of habitat will produce species and sport that, to an extent, is localized. The higher reaches of the fast-flowing rivers will support trout, with grayling as the species more often taken by coarse-fishing techniques. Lower down, where the river deepens, dace, chub and barbel will begin to appear. Many small fish species also live in this region but they are of little angling importance. As fish increase in numbers, the predators also appear in the river. Pike and perch live by hunting smaller species in the fast river. Then they seek the quiet backwaters, where they can escape the full force of the current flow but strike from suitable ambush points.

As the flow eases, and the river both deepens and widens, the most important of all our river species, the roach, is found. Soon the fast river changes its character, slowing down to lose some of the clean sparkling runs and glides found upstream. The bream zone comes into being. This is the section in most rivers containing the bulk of available food and, naturally, the most fish species. With slack currents, the larger members of the carp family take up residence. Here we fish for bream, river carp, tench and another predator, the zander.

There is, of course, a degree of overlap between fish species and habitat. For instance, the roach can be caught in quite shallow fast water and yet it is perfectly at home in the sluggish glides of the river's lower reaches, almost to the sea. In fact, the roach is so tolerant of water types that it grows to magnificent proportions in completely stillwater lakes and ponds.

(Left) *A well-oxygenated stream*
(Below) *A slow-running river.*

A hybrid waterway

Canals offer anglers a fishing situation that is both sluggish river and stillwater in one environment. The canal has little flow when given a casual glance and yet, with the passage of even the smallest boat, the opening of lock gates will introduce enough movement to keep the water circulating. This subtle flow encourages the growth of good plantlife, oxygenates the water and allows fish to travel and so populate new areas. If there is a problem, it is that canals are fairly shallow, rarely exceeding 5 ft (1.5 m) in depth. This means they are subject to quite considerable temperature changes which can create difficult angling possibilities.

Stillwater habitats

The stillwaters of Europe vary tremendously from the tiny farm pond to huge Scottish lochs and those man-made tracts of water that industry and humans rely on for their tapwater. All contain fish, provided conditions for life-support are suitable and man seeds the infant reservoir to create a fishery. Fish eggs may also be carried there from other water on the feet of wading birds.

Small ponds

Beloved by small boys, the farm pond has been many anglers' introduction to the sport. Fish rarely grow to record sizes but, if the balance of food creatures and fish is correct, one can often catch a good specimen. Roach, rudd, bream and tench predominate, with carp often introduced as a bonus fish. The size of the pond and its depth will usually dictate just how the fishing will be. Stillwaters, of this type, are often shallow. They are affected, markedly, by changes in temperature. In winter the species contained in the pond will separate. The carp and tench hibernate throughout the colder months whereas roach and bream may still take anglers' baits. The small pond will often benefit from some judicious 'gardening'. Waterweed can easily choke this habitat, as warm water and summer sunshine promote the growth of excessive weed. The larger fish help to keep weed down by feeding among the root systems but weed control sometimes has to be helped along by the fishermen.

Sooner or later the small pond becomes too fertile. With luxuriant weed growth providing both food and cover, the inhabitants breed very successfully. If, as so often is the case, there are no predatory species present the pond becomes over-stocked with stunted fry. The quality of fishing will then diminish as the competition for food increases. Some of the fish have to be removed to other waters that may well need them. Small ponds are excellent fisheries but can be among the hardest waters to manage when a consistent quality of angling is demanded. However, as I have said, they make first-rate breeding ponds!

(Top) *Canals can be superb fisheries providing they are not subject to discharge from industrial complexes.* (Above) *In an age when stillwaters are under angling pressure, some lakes suffer from neglect. The weedbeds growing out into the lake are choking the available fishing areas.* (Right) *Even municipal lakes are capable of being extremely good fisheries.*

Park lakes

In company with most ornamental creations, fishing doesn't often figure high in the builder's priorities. The park lake has to serve the needs of suburban and city dwellers who may want to see beautiful waterfowl paddling away on the water, or even to take a leisurely row on its placid surface. Fish will be there swimming under all the commotion. They will be well fed, for these fish take all the food that drops down from the ducks' meal.

Fishing this habitat can be difficult but rewarding as the colder months of each year arrive. The folk that feed the birds still perform their task but the boat people disappear. Then we anglers can get started. Some park waters contain surprisingly large fish. Occasionally, these waters are stocked, and many an angler has slipped a goodly specimen into his local lake after showing the family a fish that travelled well in the car's boot. Possibly the only drawback to this fishing is that the banks are usually constructed of concrete or asphalt. It makes for a hard standing for the angler's pitch but with little of the naturalness of a lake deep in the open countryside. Most stillwater species will grow well in park lakes without becoming overpopulated from stunted, small fry, for the waterfowl do provide an element of predation.

Large lakes and reservoirs.

Loch Lomond in Scotland is 26 miles (42 km) long and is said to be over 600 ft (183 m) deep and yet it has something in common with a typical East Anglian water only a few acres in extent and no more than 20 ft (6 m) deep—shallows. They are the answer to our fishing possibilities. For it is in the shallow margins to any lake that the weed grows, the sun warms the water and the fish feed.

The larger the lake the more room there is for fish to establish territory. So it is inevitable that the huge waters seem to regularly

produce big fish. These vast lakes are not easy to fish. Where does one start when faced with such immense, open waters? Well, I think the answer is to look upon the lake as having a fertile strip reaching about 50 yd (46 m) out from the bank with a number of natural features along that strip. Small streams entering the lake, visible banks and channels offshore, weedbeds, in fact anything that might give fish a feeding ground or patch of security from predators will provide a starting point for the angler. Fish are not evenly spread throughout the area or depth of any lake, they have specific living requirements. So the angler that spends a little time on understanding the needs of the creatures he hunts will be well on the way to becoming both successful as a fisher and a natural historian.

Many large lakes are too deep to provide much weed growth in their deepest parts. In freshwater, sunlight cannot penetrate much below 50 ft (15 m), so fish that live there are hunting smaller fish for most of their yearly cycle. The huge brown trout that inhabit some Scottish glacial lochs are an example of this kind of feeding. But even these huge brownies come into shallows to breed, penetrating up into the loch's feeder streams. In the early months of the trout season they are sometimes slow to return to the deeps and that is when anglers can get a bait in front of the giants. It is the same with some of the newly created reservoirs. Often being flooded farmland, these waters are extremely fertile. Most of the reservoirs are given over to trout fishing but there is now a suggestion that any new ones ought to be made into coarse fisheries. I know of a large, long-established reservoir in Essex that contains huge shoals of bream and quite good pike. Unfortunately,

(Below left) *This Irish lough has specimen trout and pike.*

(Below left) *Immature fry live in weedbeds.* (Below) *Brown trout.*

anglers are only allowed access to a relatively small part of the bank so there is considerable difficulty in contacting the fish. Multi-usage of public water undertakings demands that anglers must learn to live with dinghy-sailers and birdwatchers. We need the water so must make the attempt to observe other people's needs.

Gravel pits

Over the years man has dug many holes in the ground to remove ores, minerals and gravels. When these pits first appeared they were rightly cursed as hazards to young people and animals but we've learned to live with them and the angling fraternity have cause to applaud their happening. With the angling population explosion of the late 1960s, pressure on freshwater was such that many intending followers of the sport could find no fishing. The gravel pits, dug so extensively as the building programme of post-war years demanded, were now becoming naturalized. They weren't required as receptacles for city rubbish, so lay unused in close proximity to most of our major towns.

Nature has a way of seeding such waters with fish. Whether birds carry the spawn on their feet into enclosed waters, or men slip the fish into the water matters not. The fact is that many of these gravel pits have become leading fisheries. They rarely have even depths, so weed growth gets a foothold and just a few years gives the angler a fishery with cover and a landscape that can be pleasant to sit and contemplate. Every week, a gravelpit owner comes to realize that he may well be under-employing a leisure facility—water!

(Above) *Reservoirs are intended to hold water for all domestic and industrial uses. Now, the demand for outdoor recreational activities has brought fishing and boating to the reservoir, but at times the two activities conflict.* (Left) *What was once a hole in the ground has become a pleasant-looking addition to the Essex landscape as well as a model pit fishery.* (Right) *This fishery was gouged from the Nottinghamshire countryside. Now Muskam is highly regarded among Midlands coarse anglers.*

(Above) *The Trent is fished by float fishing or by legering to explore the deep mid-river possibilities.* (Left) *Coarse fishing rods: Left to right: 12ft (3.5 m) fibreglass float rod, 10ft (3 m) swingtipper, 10ft (3 m) stepped-up carp rod, 13ft (4 m) carbonfibre matchrod and a 9ft (2.5 m) swingtipper.*

COARSE FISHING TACKLE

The sport of coarse fishing involves an enormous amount of tackle, rods and reels. The styles and fishing situations vary from county to county, with further local variations from river to river. You will hear people talk about fishing this or that river 'Trent Style', which means that they are intent on using trotting methods with tackle that has been developed for the conditions found on that mighty river of the English Midlands.

Similarly, one can find items of fishing tackle, floats and reels and even rods that bear the name of a particular river—Avon, Trent or Thames. This angling tackle has been designed to satisfy the demand for something that could cope with a water flow or casting requirement. Centrepin reels were popular on Midland rivers and were especially favoured by Sheffield fishermen. This reel allowed superb control of a trotted bait but presented some difficulty in casting the float over a distance. So the locals developed a style of casting which became known as the Nottingham cast. The introduction of the fixed-spool reel changed all that. Though easier to cast with, control was slightly haphazard. Today, the closed-face fixed spool has improved control of trotted terminal tackle to the point where most matchmen now use the reel exclusively.

Rods for running-water fishing

Modern coarse fishing rods are manufactured from hollow fibreglass tubes. Cane rods have all but disappeared from the tackle shops, although some anglers are still using their favourite rods made some years ago. Occasionally one can find a specialist rod maker who will produce a 'one off' for the specimen hunter. Many anglers doubted that the fibreglass rod could ever match the characteristic action of built cane. Certainly, the first efforts in glass left something to be desired; but today

(Left) *The Mitchell fixed-spool reel is a byword among coarse anglers.* (Right) *For trouble-free casting, spool loading must be correct. Load the nylon to $\frac{1}{8}$ in (3 mm) below the spool lip. Too little will increase friction and cut casting distance. Too much can result in coils of nylon being dragged off to snag in the butt ring and ruin the cast.*

we can duplicate cane action and go much further into building rods that can handle all our freshwater fish. Fibreglass is light in the hand, virtually unbreakable when used correctly and impervious to conditions of humidity and temperature that plagued the built-cane rod.

The trotting rod

Trotting, sometimes called 'Long-trotting', involves fishing at distance where the float is run down the river to take a bait to fish that could be 20–30 yd (20–30 m) downstream of the angler. To strike home the hook at that range, calls for a rod capable of picking up the line, overcoming the nylon's inherent stretch yet still having enough power to set the hook. Action is called for: from butt to tip the trotting rod must flex.

A sharp movement of the wrist and forearm will cause the rod to lift. An in-built, softish action keeps the middle section of the rod moving back over the angler's shoulder. Movement speeds up in the rod with the tip speeding back. From a strong arm movement, all this action joins in lifting the line clear of the water, then down to the hook. Fast-tapered rods cannot work in the same way. They would demand an exaggerated

(Above left) *An angler's rod curves as a pike fights for freedom.* (Above) *How to control line while long-trotting with a centrepin. The little finger hovers above the rim of the drum, ready to jam down at the moment of strike.* (Left) *Seymo rings have unbreakable centres; a high profile makes them ideal for matchrods.*

sweep of the arm, for it is only the tip that has very much flexibility.

Trotting rods need to be reasonably lengthy—11–12 ft (3.5 m) is usual. This will give adequate control over a wide arc, either side of the downstream track of the float, with enough length to absorb the strength of large fish and subdue them. These are important factors to keep in mind. Go for a rod that has plenty of quality rings, for long-trotting means a lot of wet nylon to lift and re-cast. Rings keep line away from the rod blank where wet line sticks, destroying casting distance and accuracy.

Float and match rods

These rods are intended for the many styles and situations found when fishing flowing water with a float. The rods vary in length depending upon the type of fish, fishing distance to be cast or size of the river. Inevitably, long rods will cast farther than short rods. Fishing close-in under the rod tip, swimming the stream or trotting on small streams call for a rod of about 11 ft (3.3 m). This will subdue quite large fish, say chub of up to 4 lb (2 kg), small barbel or weighty bream. Casting farther needs a longer rod although its strength may only be suitable to handle the same size of fish.

Match fishing, so called, really means fishing in a competitive way against other anglers. It does not mean fishing for small fish or species. Obviously matchmen need to catch whatever is in front of them so they have developed rods that will handle small fish easily, be quick on the strike and yet give them reasonable control over those large fish that happen to take the offered bait. Match rods can be any length, from 12 to 15 ft (3.5–4.5 m) depending on the angler, his style and what he

Most Dutch coarse fishers use a pole. These anglers are fishing on the Oranje Canal, near Emmen, one of Holland's many waterways.

already knows about a particular water. Matchmen demand lightness in the rod because they may be holding it for all of a four- or five-hour match. They prefer a fastish taper because of the speed in setting the hook. Some of the match-fishing environments produce only small fish. Canals, which are favourite match-fishing waters, have demanded a match rod with a difference—ultra-light to handle small fish and fine tackle. Terminal hook rigs of $\frac{3}{4}$ lb (350 g) breaking strain (b.s.) and tiny canal floats mean little weight to pull line off the reel when casting.

Pole fishing, once popular on the Thames and other rivers, is enjoying a resurgence of popularity. Continental anglers, particularly the French, have so developed the art of fishing a tight line that it has become a leading match fishing method. The pole can be used to advantage when swimming the stream on fairly slow-flowing waters. Used with an elastic shock absorber, between pole tip and fixed line length, the style can cope with quite large fish. Although stiff in action for speed on the strike, the length of a pole, which can be of any size up to 30 ft (9 m) or so, has enough flexibility in handling to smooth out sudden movements by hooked fish. After playing to the surface, hooked fish are brought within grasping range by dismantling the pole, section by section, or by collapsing one made of telescoping sections.

Most coarse fishing rods have a fully-corked handle. It's nice to hold, warm in cold weather and gives a perfect grip in wet weather. The reel is mounted on the rod using two sliding, knurled fittings. These should be a tight fit to give a secure clamping of the reel stem. Balance of the tackle in the hand depends on a number of factors: the kind of reel and its weight, position of the reel on the handle and the point of balance built into the rod by its manufacturer. I like to have my rods balanced to give a

Shock absorber

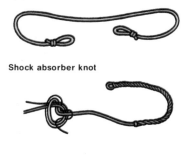

Shock absorber knot

(Left) *Many pole anglers employ an aluminium crook on the end of the pole, with a quick-release slot for attaching the elastic shock-absorbing link. It can be joined by using the knot shown.*
(Right) *Float roads have high-profile rings to keep wet nylon away from the rod. Leger rods have low-profile rings, for leger weights pull wet nylon through without friction or sticking.*
(Far right) *Two fibreglass joints.*

little weight just forward of my right hand. The balance point can easily be adjusted by weighting the rod handle at the butt with lead shots. I do this by taking off the butt cap and filling the end of the blank with SSG shots until correct balance has been achieved. Then the lead shots are permanently secured by packing them in with epoxy glue.

When he makes a rod, no manufacturer can ascertain what your balance needs are. So all rods may need and will benefit from a degree of personalization. Obviously, you will have to keep the same rod-reel combination together to preserve perfect balance.

Rods for legering

Leger rods are generally shorter than their float fishing counterparts. They are made to handle fish of a larger size range and to cast leger weights that can vary between two or three SSG and a $\frac{1}{2}$ oz (14 g) bomb lead. Indeed, pike leger rods are capable of casting a herring which may well weigh $\frac{1}{2}$ lb (225 g) or more!

The standard leger rod would be about 10 ft (3 m) in length, with a medium action falling somewhere between the all-through movement of a trotting rod and the stiffness of a fast-tapered float rod. The rings are low in profile but stronger in the wire. The ferrules (joints between sections of a rod) are spigotted, though some rods are appearing with glass-to-glass follow-on ferrules that are said to preserve the action of a rod even more than the commonly-used glass spigot. Apart from pike and carp rods, leger rods have a tip ring that incorporates an internally threaded tube into which swingtips and quivertips can be screwed. These are bite indicators used at the tip of the rod whereas carp rod anglers use more sophisticated devices that normally fit near to the reel or butt ring of the rod.

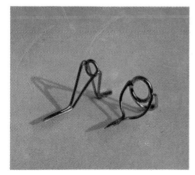

Measuring a rod's test curve.
Hold the butt (A–B) against a
wall. Pass heavy line through
the rings from the handle. Tie
on an accurate spring balance
(C). Pull the rod down to a
right-angle (D). Check the
reading and multiply by 5 to
obtain the optimum line b.s. for
the rod.

Manufacturers' descriptions for rods

It is extremely difficult for any rod maker to give an adequate description of his product. What does a leger or float rod mean in terms of what it can do and which fish species it can handle? Anglers need a simple method and terminology that means something in fishing terms, so makers now state the 'test curve' for a rod. This means the amount of pull, measured in pounds (or kilograms), necessary to pull the tip over at right angles to the handle. A test curve of, say, 1 lb (0.5 kg) is multiplied by 5 to give the line strength balanced to that particular rod—in this case 5 lb (2.25 kg). The system isn't perfect by any means but it is a starting point by which to judge the use to which a rod can be put. However, fast tapers and compound tapers built into a rod will alter the test curve as a reliable standard. With so many variations of taper and action, manufacturers would serve anglers better by stating a range of line-breaking strains for each of their products.

Spinning rods

These are really casting instruments, where the action and casting ability is probably of more importance than the actual function of playing or landing a fish. This statement may sound a trifle odd, but think about it for a moment. A spinning rod spends most of its working life casting, not landing fish. The rod needs to be able to cast effectively and with accuracy. Therefore, the rod must have programmed power,

Plummet weights. One is
attached to the end of a float rig
and lowered into the swim. The
float will sink out of sight or lay
flat on the surface. The float
must be adjusted accordingly.

The principle of the fixed-spool reel is that line peels off the spool at right angles to the rod axis. Little weight is needed to cast, for there is no friction from a revolving drum.

certainly enough to cast a range of artificial lures that may differ in weight. I prefer a blank that has sufficient 'steel', based on a relatively fast taper, to flick a bait out with a speedy tip action. Then there must be a build up of strength farther down the blank that gives its fish-playing effectiveness

A rod suitable for average trout, perch and small pike would be 8 ft (2.5 m) long with rings graduated from butt to tip that smooth the coils out from the line as it runs off the spool. Hard chrome and Fuji rings are a good investment as they stand up to constant use. The Fuji ring is particularly good for reducing friction in casting and playing a fish. Larger fish need a stronger and longer rod to give precise control when handling a powerful fighter. They are normally double-handed rods of around 10 ft (3 m) in length. There is a further use for the spinning rod and that is for the sea angler who spins from a rocky shoreline. Here, casting ability and control are vitally necessary as added to the strength of the fish is the power of current or angry seas.

Fixed-spool reels

Undoubtedly, the fixed-spool reel is the most popular type in use today. Basically, it works by line pulling off the spool that is set at right angles to the axis of the rod. To cast, the bale arm is opened and it stays open while casting. The line is prevented from spilling off the spool by the angler pressing his finger onto the spool, or the line can be picked up on

Line is picked up by the finger before the bale arm is opened. At the moment of maximum casting effort the finger is removed to allow the line to flow freely away from the spool.

the index finger. The rod is swung to make the cast and at the correct moment the finger is straightened, letting the line run free. When the cast has been made, the bale arm is closed by a turn of the reel handle. This prevents more line escaping.

Line is retrieved by winding the handle, which causes the bale arm to revolve around the spool. Internal gearing drives the spool forwards and backwards, with a pump action, that lays even layers of nylon from front to back across the width of the spool. Because line is returned to the spool through a right angle, at the pick-up point, there is an element of friction. Quality reels smooth the travel of the line using a roller incorporated within the bale arm. There has always been one major drawback in using a fixed spool. When casting into a strong head wind, especially when using a light terminal rig, line tends to blow back in coils, sometimes getting trapped in the gap between the spool and the flyer housing. A chenile insert was built around the circumference of the spool which went some way to curing the problem.

The designers then came up with a completely different concept in fixed spool reels—the skirted spool reel. This improvement in fixed spool reel design totally prevents the line getting behind the spool, because the outer flange of the spool completely shrouds the flyer housing. Some reels have no complicated bale arm closing device, which is sometimes a blessing. The new-style reel uses a simple 'knock on' bale arm which is noisy but effective.

Centrepin reels

Though not as popular as they once were, the centrepin still has a function in modern angling. Trotting demands a reel with perfect control over the line running off from the spool. Because a centrepin is only a drum running on a spindle, set at right angles to the axis of the rod, line is drawn directly off the drum and up through the rod rings. There is little friction and with quality bearings a reel can be made that turns freely with only the gentle pull of a light float trotting downstream. The angler strikes by jamming his little finger onto the rim of the drum. Playing the fish is direct and positive. A fast rate of line retrieve can be had by 'batting' the reel rim, using the palm of the hand. If there is a drawback in using a centrepin it must be that the reel is difficult to cast with. Some distance can be had by drawing off a number of loops of line, one to each finger on the free hand. Doing this will give a cast of about 24 ft (7 m).

Fishing lines

Only monofilament nylon is used as the reel line in present day fishing. Occasionally one will see an angler spinning, with a multiplying reel,

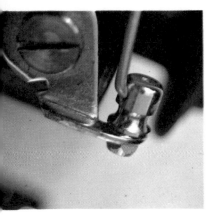

All good fixed-spool reels have a line roller incorporated in the bale arm assembly. It reduces friction as line is retrieved. (Below) *One of the problems of the fixed-spool reel was line becoming tangled behind the drum. The skirted spool has overcome this nuisance.*

The ideal trotting reel, a centre-pin, retains direct contact with fish. Line runs smoothly off the reel, pulled by current flow. (Below) *Casting with a centrepin is an art. Line drawn off the drum is held in strands by fingers. In expert hands 24 ft (7 m) can be released on casting.*

using fine braided Terylene but this line is becoming unfashionable. Nylon is the best material, almost indestructible in use and cheap to buy. Made from a synthetic polymeric amide, monofilament nylon is said to be as strong as mild steel of the same gauge. But nylon doesn't last forever: it can fail without warning especially when the reel is left exposed to strong sunlight, for ultra-violet light has a weakening effect. So play safe and use your line for a season, then replace it.

Nylon varies in line strength for a given diameter from maker to maker. What the fisherman needs is the strongest line with the smallest diameter. Colour is something that all anglers argue about. We do not really know whether fish can see nylon clearly *or* whether they ignore a suspended line because hunger for the attached bait overcomes their wariness. Nevertheless, I have found that a neutral grey *seems* to be a colour that works if it isn't too highly polished. I suppose that under certain conditions of penetrating sunlight it glints in the water.

Average breaking strain × diameter
(dry breaking strain)

in	mm	lb	kg
0.003	0.08	1.0	0.50
0.004	0.10	1.5	0.70
0.005	0.12	2.0	0.90
0.006	0.15	3.0	1.4
0.007	0.17	4.0	1.8
0.008	0.20	5.5	2.5
0.009	0.22	7.0	3.2
0.010	0.25	9.0	4.0
0.011	0.28	11.0	5.0
0.012	0.30	12.5	5.7

Hooks for freshwater fishing

There are a multitude of differing hook patterns. Mustad, the Norwegian hook makers, list over one thousand hooks and each of these is made in many sizes! Obviously they aren't all intended for the sport of fishing. Most of the hooks will be made for the commercial fishing industry. In choosing the correct hook to use one must ask several questions:

1. What size and kind of bait will I be using?
2. What species of fish do I intend catching?
3. Should I buy loose hooks or those already tied to nylon lengths?

Hook size must relate to bait size. A 16 hook is suitable for one maggot; bread flake is held securely on a No. 12 hook.

The size of hook chosen is dictated by the kind of bait. Maggots or casters, fished as a single or double bait, will call for a smallish hook, say about size 16, whereas a large piece of flake needs to be moulded around a larger hook of size 12 proportions. It is both a question of whether the bait would be split by the thickness of the wire and whether the bait will stay on the hook during the cast. At the same time we must match a hook to the size of the fish that are likely to be caught. A carp of 10 lb (3 kg) or so will need a fairly strong hook. So we choose a pattern known for its strength and in a size that will hold and be hidden within the chosen bait.

At least two or three patterns of freshwater hook, tied to nylon lengths or droppers, are available from each fishing tackle manufacturer. Usually, these hooks are of the spade-end type and the nylon varies between 12 in (30 cm) and 36 in (1 m) in length. The tackle makers ensure that the hooks are tied on with good knots to nylon with a breaking strain that varies according to the size of the hook. For example

> Size 6 is tied to 7 lb (3.2 kg) b.s. nylon
> Size 8 is tied to 5 lb (2 kg) b.s. nylon
> Size 10 is tied to 4 lb (1.8 kg) b.s. nylon
> Size 12 is tied to 3 lb (1.4 kg) b.s. nylon
> Size 14 is tied to 2.5 lb (1 kg) b.s. nylon
> Size 16 is tied to 2 lb (1 kg) b.s. nylon
> Size 18 is tied to 1.5 lb (0.7 kg) b.s. nylon
> Size 20 is tied to 1.5 lb (0.7 kg) b.s. nylon

These breaking strains are average but do not suit all anglers. Many prefer to tie their own hooks to suit the fishing or their style.

Size chart for Mustad-Crystal, forged, spade-end hooks. From No. 1, hooks get smaller down to size 20. From size 1/0 they get larger up to 12/0 or more.

Mustad-Crystal forged spade-end hooks

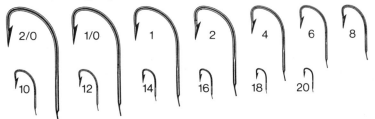

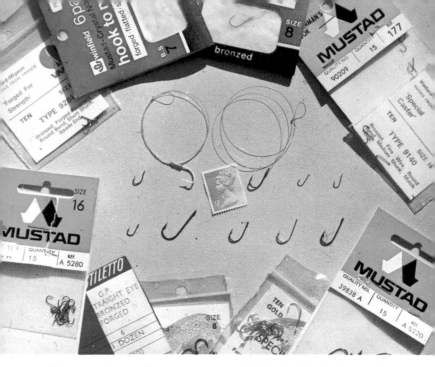

There are few requirements to a good fish hook. The hook must be as strong as it can be made without becoming excessively thick in the metal. The point must be sharp, for perfect penetration, with a neat barb that gives adequate holding power. If forged, the temper ought to be such that the hook will give a little to the pull of a powerful fish. It must not snap or straighten. Any hook will fail if it isn't balanced to the line and the built-in power of the rod. Imagine a situation where a fine-wire size 16 hook is tied to 6 lb (2.75 kg) nylon and then used on a stepped-up carp rod. Something has got to give when a big fish is being played. You can bet that it will be the hook! Similarly, with a light rod and line one would have difficulty pulling a size 2 carp hook into the jaw of a big specimen.

Leads for freshwater fishing

Freshwater fishing leads fall into two distinct kinds: those that are nipped onto the nylon, and leads that are tied on. In float fishing we rely on split shot, that can come in a variety of sizes and shapes. At one time anglers used only the round split shot that came into angling from the

(Left) *Just a few of the thousands of hook patterns available.* (Right) *There is a wide choice of weights for float and leger fishing. Here are two kinds of split shot, an Arlesey bomb, plain sinker lead, coffin, bullet and barrel leads that slide onto the line, and two forms of Newark leger pin weights.* (Below) *Three varieties of split lead weights, some conventional split shot, a Styl lead, and 'mouse droppings'.*

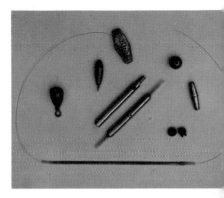

shotgun cartridge industry, but nowadays new shapes have evolved that give less resistance to the pull of a fish and possibly have a better aerodynamic shape for casting. Split shot should be made from the softest lead available so that it can be gently pinched onto the line. Hard lead needs to be gripped vigorously to close the slice, but in so doing often cuts through the nylon. Look for split shot that has a fairly deep cut that is central to the body of the lead. Avoid uneven slicing that is also likely to be offset.

Leads have a unique size system that doesn't quite reduce in even steps. However, many float makers give a shot-loading for their products and it isn't too difficult to learn the loading for the rest of the floats that are in your tackle box.

SPLIT SHOT SIZE and number per oz (28 g)

SSG	AAA	BB	1
15	35	70	100

3	4	5	6	7	8
140	170	220	270	340	450

shot shown actual size

Often you will find a shot-loading given as $2\frac{1}{2}$ BB for a particular float. Match anglers are especially fond of using this terminology. It really means that the float will cock, to the makers' recommended line, at a shot load of 2 BB + 1 No. 3.

Leger weights

There are four basic kinds of leger weight used in modern coarse angling. Each lead serves a different purpose in that some are intended to hold bottom against strong current flow, while others are made to move with the water so that baits can be rolled across the bottom of a river or stream.

The coffin lead, with its acute edges, can be used to fish a static bait. The hard corners are made to grip into the mud and gravel that form a river bed. The reel line is threaded through the body of the lead where it is supposed to slide, freely, through to the bite of a taking fish. Unfortunately, the hole is easily clogged up by the minute detritus that is constantly swept across the lead by the current flow. The coffin, barrel and bullet leads all have this problem and added to this they are not good leads for casting. Because there is no centre of gravity, these weights tend to tumble through the air causing the hook link to become tangled.

Richard Walker, captor of the official British record carp, gave fresh-water anglers a new leger weight that flies true during the cast *and* rolls effectively across a river without tangling the hook link. Called the Arlesey Bomb, the design puts the weight at the head of the lead and incorporates a swivel to run the reel line through.

(Left) *Make the link leger by pinching SSG shot onto a short nylon loop.* (Below) *Spinning leads and an anti-kink device. They should be used above the swivel connecting the reel line to the spinning trace. Left to right: anti-kink vane, fold-over lead, Hillman lead, Wye lead and spiral lead (bottom).*

Split shots can be used to construct a leger weight. They are simply linked together on a short piece of nylon which is folded over the reel line. The nylon link leger, as it is called, has two valuable features: it slides easily, and if the weights should go fast into the bottom a steady pull will cause the shots to pull off the short link. The advantage is that the breakout involves only the loss of a couple of SSG shots.

Spinning weights

Many of the artificial lures that form a part of the coarse fisher's armoury need just a little extra lead to get them out to any distance over the water. Spinning leads are attached about 3 ft (1 m) up from the lure. They have an additional function in that they help to remove the twist that some spinners put into the reel line. Fixed above the trace swivel, the lead prevents the twisting motion passing beyond the swivel.

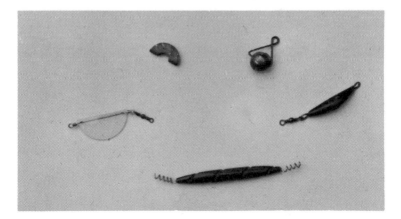

(Left) *Carp fishing can often be a waiting game in the dark. This makes bite detection difficult as bobbin indicators are not visible. The electronic bite indicator is triggered as the fish pulls the line against a spring lever. The slightest movement of the line results in a loud buzzing sound and a flashing light – both combining to arouse the sleepy angler!* (Right) *Tidiness and protection are given by this strongly built floatbox. Split shot and leger weights are arranged in the segmented rear compartment, and there is a large selection of floats easily to hand in the front of the box.*

There are three or four varieties of spinning, anti-kink weight. The Wye can be purchased with or without a swivel, the banana-shape acts as an anti-kink keel. I like to fit the lead with a quick-release swivel at both ends of the weight, enabling me to change lures and weight of spinning lead without constantly having to retie my knots. I must admit to not liking the Jardine or spiral lead. It is easily bent to form an anti-kink shape but mine always seem to come off during the cast. I wind the nylon around the lead correctly but, nevertheless, it comes adrift. I have been told, many times, to squeeze up the spiral wires to stop the nylon escaping but surely that defeats the object of an efficient, quick-release system? Possibly less well known today, but equally useful, are the half-moon fold-over leads and the Hillman spinning lead. I believe that they are perfect for the light tackle spinner, the man who is winkling out trout from a small stream.

Bite detectors

Detecting a bite from a feeding fish can be made in any number of ways. Certainly, three human senses are brought into play: (a) sight, where we rely on floats and devices that are fixed onto the rod, (b) sound, as given out by the electronic equipment so loved by the carp fisherman and other specimen hunters, and (c) touch as used by the leger angler as he

patiently sits with his line held between his fingers waiting for the tiniest tremble on the line.

Floats are by far the most important item of bite detection used by coarse fishers. Look into any angler's basket and you will find a float box packed with favourites and floats that are a delight to own but are never used! A float has two functions; it gives visual indication of a bite but, more importantly, it supports the bait at a fixed level in the water and will also carry a bait to an area where fish are known to be.

Floats are made from a number of natural substances and, in recent years, from man-made materials. Each material has a function that makes it important to the angler. Balsa wood is extremely light in weight and can carry a sizable shot loading as it is such a buoyant substance. Reeds, formerly gathered from places like the Norfolk Broads but now

Floats can be made from a large number of materials. Left to right: balsa wood dowel, cane dowel, peacock quill and sacandas reed. Other materials are reed, cork and plastic.

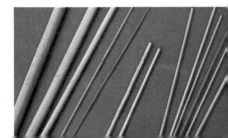

brought from the marshy places in Pakistan and India, have great buoyancy with a natural hardened casing. They also have good buoyant characteristics, capable of carrying heavy shot loads, with a natural regularity of size which makes for easy manufacture. A lot of our modern floats have a stem, sometimes to act as an antenna and often to give a float length without increasing its buoyancy at all. Cane is the most acceptable material to form stems; it is light and immensely strong yet there is little inherent buoyancy.

Polystyrene moulded bodies have appeared among floats, mainly those made on the Continent and a few from Japan. It is a good material, both light and inexpensive but the bodies are easily crushed and there is some difficulty in applying the necessary paint to give the float an attractive appearance and to seal the polystyrene. There are complete ranges of moulded plastic floats, which ought to become popular as they are cheap and well made. The problem is that anglers are steeped in tradition and will not accept that plastic is a useful substance from which to make floats.

I suppose that natural quills will never lose their place in freshwater fishing. The porcupine quill is one of nature's finest offerings to the angler. It is totally waterproof and is available in a variety of sizes. Both as a trotting and stillwater float, it will perform beautifully with just the addition of a painted tip and whipped-on ring.

The birds, of both field and sea, provide us with another source of quills. The crow, swan and gull all drop flight feathers that can be used to make light, buoyant stillwater floats. Very little work is needed to make a quill. The feather must be trimmed off using a sharp razor blade. Then the quill is given a light rub along the line of the feather joinings with fine glass paper. Don't rub too hard otherwise you will destroy the natural hardening glaze that feather quills have, making the float take in water. Rings can either be made from fine gauge brass wire or 20 lb (10 kg) nylon. Whip the ring on with fine thread. The whipping should be fixed with a fine coating of waterproof glue before varnishing. This will prevent the ring from pulling away from the base of the quill.

A few years ago, float-making was an extension of the art of angling.

(Top right) *Floats for still and running water. Left to right: porcupine, dart, onion, light Avon, heavy Avon, ducker, sliding antenna, zoomer, stick, trotter.*

(Right) *Pole floats of balsa and sacandas reed on wire stems. The plastic winders hold made-up pole-fishing casts wound on the frame with float, hook and shot.*

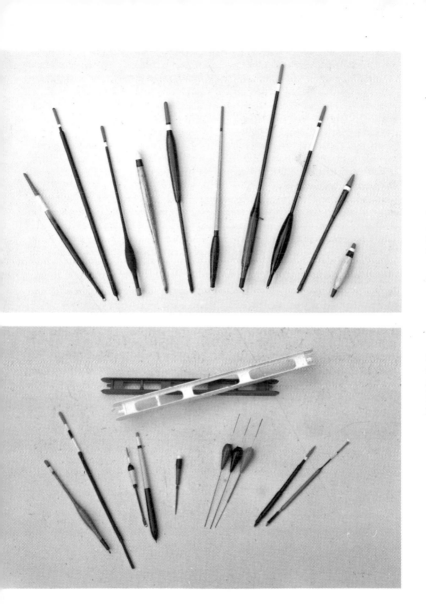

37

All manner of strange materials was used in the construction of floats. As an example, anglers who specialized in trotting made float bodies from elder pith. It is a tremendously buoyant substance but so fragile that constant breakages prompted the angler to use something more robust. One material that has almost disappeared from quality floats is cork. A standby material for so many industries, it has been in such demand that rod makers have had a hard time getting enough close-grained cork to make rod handles, let alone float bodies. It appears that women's platform shoes and bathroom tiles took all the good cork available. Even wine bottles have to suffer plastic stoppers!

Rod tip bite indicators
Of all the on-rod indicators, the swingtip and quivertip must now be the most popular. Simple in use and construction, they do not require the angler to leave his box or seat to set after each cast. Both versions are really intended for fishing situations where big fish *that run* are not expected. The swingtip, brainchild of tackle dealer Jack Clayton, is fundamentally a swinging arm carrying a couple of rod rings and fitted with a flexible joint to the rod.

The connection is made with a threaded boss that screws into a Hopton-type rod tip ring. Most float and light leger rods are today fitted

The swingtip is an ideal bite indicator for still and slow-running water. Set the tip to 45°. There are two kinds of bite indication: a rising swingtip means a fish is moving away; if the arm swings towards the rod tip a fish is heading towards the angler.

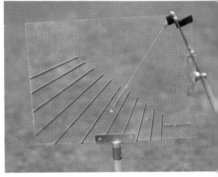

According to the fishing style, floats can be attached by top rubber and bottom ring (Avon), bottom rubber (dart), or by using two split shot to lock the float depth (ducker or zoomer).

A sight board can be very useful for detecting crafty bites. It is a boon on a windy day when the swingtip is blown about, thus spoiling accurate bite detection by normal visual means.

with this style of tip ring. The flexible joint is either of rubber or plastic. I prefer rubber (as for valve tubes) because it doesn't stiffen up in cold weather. Plastic tubes suffer from variations in flexibility under different temperature conditions. The swinging arm can be made of hard nylon rod, cane, solid fibreglass rod or aluminium rod, such as a knitting needle. Try to get one with two rings, a support intermediate and a centred tip ring, which will ease the flow of line out through the rings when casting.

Length of the swingtip arm can be important. One of over 12 in (30 cm) becomes unmanageable when casting. A 10 in (26 cm) arm is about right and can be made from several weights of material to give a range of sensitivity under different wind conditions, for a stiff breeze is the bane of all swingtips. It dances the tip around, making bite detection almost impossible. There are two ways to partially overcome the effect of wind. One is to protect the swingtip with a sight board that shelters the rod tip from the prevailing wind. The other is to load the tip with additional weight, either added SSG shots or wrapped-round lead wire, but both of these methods will dull the sensitivity of the detector. Of course, strong current flow will also affect the usefulness of a swingtip and it is under these conditions we use the quiver tip.

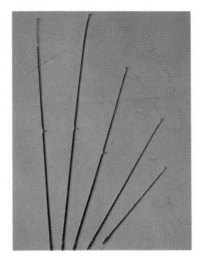

(Left) *Quivertips are used for bite detection in running water when wind makes a swingtip hard to use. They come in different lengths and vary in sensitivity.* (Right) *A springtip is used in the same way as a quivertip. It registers bites by bending from the spring coils, not along its length. For shy-biting fish the springtip is hard to beat.* (Far right) *Indicators can be made from dough or plastic and are fixed near the rod butt. They are best used when fish bite strongly or on species such as carp that make positive runs after taking a bait.*

Quivers are made from springy rods, and can be either metal or glass fibre. The idea is that the quivertip is screwed into the threaded tip ring and becomes a sensitive extension to the rod tip. Being much finer in diameter than the rod blank, the quiver will react to the tiniest pull from a feeding fish. Both the swingtip and quivertip are set for use in the same way. The cast is made and the leger weight is given time to settle on the bed of the river or lake. Then the line is slowly wound in until there is a tight line between rod and weight. The line is then relaxed to leave the indicators in the positions shown in the illustration. By settling the swinging or sprung arm slightly under tension one can get an indication of two kinds of bite. A pull-away bite will raise the swinging arm or pull the quivertip forward, whereas a fish that mouths the bait and moves toward the angler will cause the swingtip to drop back to the vertical position and the quivertip to lie straight.

Quivertips can be made in a number of spring tensions: fairly stiff, for strong current, and relatively springy for fishing in the quiet waters of a gentle streamy water. The spring tension must be judged to suit both power of current and hook shyness of the fish species.

Rod butt bite detectors

The old dough bobbin must surely rank as the first of this kind of bite indicator. Simple but effective, it is attached to the reel line between the reel and the first rod ring. The weight of the bobbin again has to be

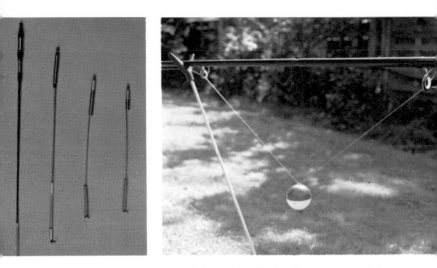

adjusted to suit the current and the fish whilst having enough weight to hang down on the V of nylon. If there is a fault with the butt indicator it is that there is considerable friction when a fish pulls line through the rings against the weighted bobbin. Wary fish will feel resistance to their bite and possibly drop the bait. Fred Buller, author of the definitive book on pike fishing, suggests placing the bobbin on the line after it leaves the tip ring. Here the indicator acts as a swingtip. The only difference in use is that the angler has to leave his seat after each cast to place the bobbin onto the reel line. Dough bobbins, so called, can be easily made from a bulbous float fitted with a ladies hairgrip. There are simpler forms of butt indicator. A piece of silverpaper folded over the line is very popular. One thing more—tie the bobbin, whenever it is used, on to the bankstick with a length of line. You would be surprised how difficult it is to find a bobbin that flies off when you strike into the bite!

The rod tip itself can be a bite indicator. Many years ago my bite detection, when legering, was a mixture of watching for trembles on the rod tip and feeling for bites while holding the line between thumb and finger. It was a good system for running water and was surprisingly sensitive. Without doubt, one reacts much faster to a vibration felt through the fingers than to a movement that is seen!

In stillwater, the simplest form of bite detection is to allow a slightly

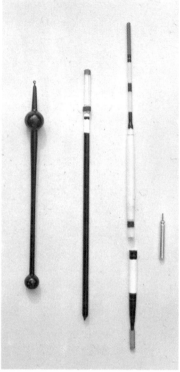

(Above) *Split shots with moulded fingergrips which can be squeezed on and off the line.* (Right) *Some illuminated floats employ a tiny battery to light a bulb; others have a glowing tube claimed to remain luminous for years. The odd-shaped leger weight has a buoyant top for keeping the line above weedy bottoms.* (Below) *The best keepnet must be the largest you can afford. Minnow mesh will not damage fish providing the net is not overfilled. Never shake the fish down to the mouth of the net. That is when fins and scales become damaged.*

slack line connection between the legered tackle and rod tip. A taking fish will easily straighten the line without feeling any resistance at all. But one must have extremely good eyesight.

Carp fishing has become a specialized part of coarse fishing. Indeed, carp fishermen have brought the business of bite detection to a fine art. The merest tremble on the line is picked up by devices that rely on electrical contact to produce an audible or visual warning of a fish's interest in the bait. Carp are notoriously shy in their methods of feeding. They seem to detect the drag of a float or leger weight all too easily, so baits are offered that do not have the addition of weight to get casting distance. The line is allowed to settle and then is passed across a trembler. Any pull, however slight, activates a buzzer or switches a light on. Both warning systems are necessary because carp fishing is often undertaken in the hours of darkness. One can use less sophisticated ways of detecting a biting fish; the dough bobbin can be set to drag across a sheet of newspaper creating a rustle that will be heard in the dead of night.

Some bobbins are available that use a form of light given off by a harmless radiation cell. The difficulty in using them is that, in pitch darkness, one has difficulty in judging whether they have in fact moved at all! What is really needed is to use two: a fixed light and a bobbin, then it becomes easier to judge movement between two light sources.

Two more luminous bite systems remain: a conventional torch which can be positioned to shine on the bobbin or out across the water to a float, and the float that has its own light and power source from a light-emitting diode (LED). I've used one recently while tench fishing. It was really good because the float could be set for accurate depth before the last of the evening light disappeared. Then, with just the glowing tip above the water surface, bite detection was immediate because the light went out the moment the float-dipped. The floats are expensive although the batteries, lithium cells, last for 15 hours as there is little current drain to the LED.

The coarse fisher's nets

There have been tremendous advances in net manufacture in recent years. Gone are the rough, knotted, hard nylon nets that did so much damage to fish, scraping the protective slime and scales from their bodies. Today we have soft, knitted netting that is both kind to fish and long-lasting.

Keepnets

The best keepnet is the largest one you can afford of the best quality available. A net is subjected to hard usage, continually in the water, being dragged up over rough banks with—perhaps—a lot of fish within it. A $6\frac{1}{2}$ ft (2 m) net is the smallest feasible size because it is the amount of keepnet that is actually in the water that matters. From even the lowest bank a net is always partially out of the water. Fixed onto the bank stick much of its length is taken up just reaching the water.

Diameter is also important. An 18 in (50 cm) diameter net is only good for fish of about 14 in (40 cm) long. Fish don't lie along the length of a net, they have to face into whatever current there is in order to breathe. A wider net would ensure that they do not rub a nose or tail fin when moving about, and they are often on the move, jostling one another for the best lie possible. Try to keep the net extended if you can. In a slack current or in stillwater, the net will often collapse onto the fish. A sea angler's lead of about 6 oz (170 g), fixed to the bottom of the net, will help to hold it down in the flow. Some net makers can now provide a form of stick which is placed between the supporting rings to keep the net open and extended . . . a good idea for the fish!

Landing nets
Every freshwater angler should own a landing net. It is impossible to land any reasonably sized fish properly without one. The net should be made of the same soft mesh as we now have for keepnets. Quite

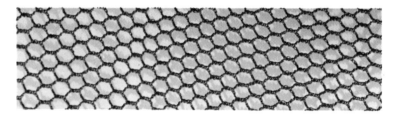

(Above) *An example of finely woven keepnet mesh. There are no knots and the material is soft and pliant.* (Left) *Barrel, link, three-way and ball-bearing swivels are used in coarse fishing and when spinning. The ball-bearing kind are especially useful to the salmon angler who places great strains upon his trace and the connecting link.*

When landing a fish, lower the net's rim into the water. Play the fish toward it while holding the rod tip high. Draw the fish over the net and lift firmly. Once trapped, the fish is secure.

obviously, the same fin and scale damage can be caused to fish if the net is not of suitable material and size.

Size of net is vitally important to the angler because many specimens have been lost when the net wasn't large enough to accommodate them. It is at the moment of netting that fish often make their last desperate attempt at gaining freedom. They will often swim in quietly but panic when they see the rim of the net. Likewise, the angler often panics and prods at the fish with the frame of the net. What needs to be done to ensure a successful netting is for the net to be lowered into the water in advance of the fish coming into the bank. Where the water is shallow, the net can be rested on the bottom. Then the fish is drawn over the net by a raising of the rod tip. As the fish's body slides across the rim, the handle is raised lifting the net rim 1 ft (30 cm). Immediately this has been accomplished the fish cannot escape the net. If the specimen is a large one, the rod can be laid down, giving the angler an opportunity to use two hands to lift the net and fish to safe ground. In my experience, one hand to the landing net handle and the other hand to the rim of the net is a good rule. A fish weighs little in water so the full weight only becomes apparent as the creature leaves its supporting element.

Extending handles are a good idea where one has to fish from banks

Match anglers use a shallow, pan-shaped landing net to speed up the operation of landing and unhooking the fish.

Fine micro-mesh netting is a boon to the leger angler. The leger weight cannot fall through and tangle in the net.

that are steep or the pitch is fairly high out of the water. Seek an extending handle with a positive locking device that prevents the handle from coming apart or revolving. A polished alloy handle can be hard to grip in cold weather, so bind some coarse twine around it.

Deep nets, about 2 ft (50 cm) or so, are perfect when fishing for the large, powerful species such as barbel, carp and pike. For general coarse fishing, a slightly shallower net is desirable as it saves delving down to find the fish, for all this activity tends to rub the body of your catch, doing possible damage. Match anglers have altered both the depth and shape of their landing nets recently. They use a very shallow net which lets them speed up the task of removing the hook. They also use a round net whereas most nets are triangular these days, due to the fact that the shape is easy to make in a folding net design. One advantage in a triangular net frame is that a lively fish, that may try to break away just as the net appears below it, finds three dark corners. The curtain of netting tends to make the fish dive down for what it takes to be security.

I like a landing net made with mini-mesh netting. It may be a little heavier to lift when sodden with water but it has a mesh that will not let leger bombs slip through. The old, open weave netting was a curse when leger weights and other terminal tackle found their way through.

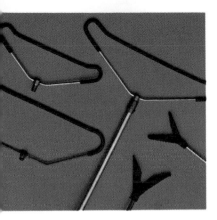 

Three stretched rubber and two V-shaped rod-rest heads, the latter giving free flow to the angler's running line.

When free-running line is vital a V-forked rod-rest head is used. The channel allows line to run through without friction.

Rod rests

In my time, I've used every form of rod rest, from a lunch basket to a forked stick cut from the nearest hedgerow. But to support the rod properly one needs at least two rests with their accompanying bank sticks. For the float fisherman the Sheffield rest, which uses a piece of rubber tubing slightly bowed between the two arms of an alloy frame, is as good as any. I can offer one improvement and that is for a hump to be incorporated on one side. This prevents the rod being blown off the rest in a side wind. The raised side can be a minor obstruction to the slashing sideways strike but it is rare. For the leger angler there is a similar type that has a central 'gutter' which allows the line to run out without being trapped on either the rubber or other material of the rod rest. Both of these rests are used toward the rod tip. At the butt, a plain 'V' fork rest will suffice though most anglers like to hold the handle of the rod across their knees for immediate reaction to a bite. Try to get rod rest heads that have a facility for inclining the head to a vertical position, even though the bank stick may be driven in at an angle.

Disgorgers

The care of fish is a responsibility of every angler. Removing the hook properly is a must and, in consequence, anglers must use a correctly

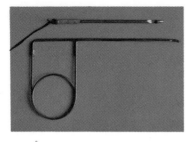

I use two disgorgers. For small fish I prefer the slotted form. It slides down the line to meet the head of the hook. Large fish demand stronger, bigger hooks which can be removed by artery forceps or a 'Valley' disgorger which has a spring-loaded removal system that disgorges without stress to the fish.

designed disgorger. If I had my way I would ban the use of the open, so-often sharp-jawed, disgorger. It is lethal in the hands of a novice where frantic probing can easily rupture the delicate membranes in the fish's throat. The result is a *dead fish*. Far better to use a slotted disgorger that is both effective and infinitely more humane.

To remove a hook, lay the disgorger onto the line with the flatted section held crosswise. Keep a slight tension on the line by holding the fish against a reasonable pull on the rod tip. You will find this easier to accomplish if the rod is laid down on the rests. Then, swivel the disgorger so that the line is picked up by the slot. A tiny wrist movement will push the slotted section down over the head of the hook. Trapping the line against the body of the disgorger will hold the hook secure. Then a gentle push will ease the hook out from its hold.

Look at the size of the slot in the head of the disgorger when you buy it. There are two sizes. One suits spade end hooks and the larger one fits over the larger head of ringed hooks.

There are many other accessories and items of fishing tackle but I will introduce them in sections with specific use.

Knots

The difference between a good knot and a bad one is often a good fish! Bad knots are unforgivable and unnecessary. Tying perfect knots, in nylon or any other line, is only a matter of learning and practice. The river bank is not the place to get the required practice. There are too many distractions and with the excitement of the occasion you will be all fingers and thumbs. May I suggest a way to get to grips with the basic knots?

Buy a few large-size angling hooks and a spool of fairly thick nylon, say 20 lb (10 kg) b.s. Now, with the book open, go through the stages of tying on each knot. Compare your effort with the illustration. Keep tying until you have the confidence to work down to the small hook sizes that are common in coarse fishing. If you have trouble with the minute size 18s, buy a hook tying device. I use one as my eyes are no longer perfect and the hand shakes.

Remember that there is no in-built safety margin when tying knots in nylon. Each knot reduces the breaking strain by a definite amount. The more knots in a particular terminal rig the weaker that contact between fish and man becomes! Always assist the knot and its coils to slide up tight by lubricating the line. This is best done by licking the loosely tied knot before drawing it tight. Pull up gradually, never snatch at the knot, this will only lead to an immediate break or, what is worse, a weakened line that parts when a fish is being played.

Knots for tying on hooks and swivels

There are two basic types of hook. One has a ringed eye, forming a metal loop to which the nylon can be tied. The tucked half-blood knot is the best knot for this pattern; it is easy to tie and preserves most of the line's breaking strain. Pass the line through the eye of the hook and twist the loose end around the standing line five times. Then, take the end back through the small V space at the eye. Now pass the line through the large loop formed. Lick the nylon and gradually pull the knot tight. That is all there is to it! Swivels, spinners and plugs can be tied on with the same knot.

Tucked half-blood knot

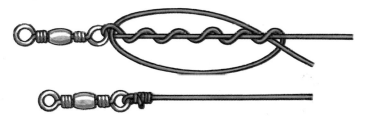

Spade end hooks do not have an eye. They are finished with a flattened head where the round wire section of the hook swells out. So what we need is a knot that will grip around the round shank of the hook. It is then slid up to butt against the swollen, flattened area. Generally, this style of hook is used for smallish fish in freshwater, so hooks are rarely above size 6. But, you will find spade end hooks used down to size 22 which is very small indeed!

49

Spade-end whipping knot

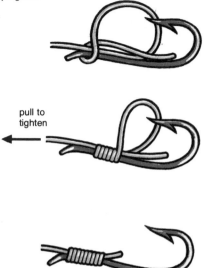

pull to
tighten

Take the hook in the fingers of the left hand, assuming that you are right handed. Lay a loop of nylon along the shank of the hook with *at least* 4 in (10 cm) of loose line left free. Pinch the hook shank and both strands of nylon between thumb and forefinger. Now bind the open loop of nylon at least six times around the shank of the hook. Pass the free end of line back through the loop at the bend of the hook. Lick the knot and gently pull on the standing line. This will cause the loop to close, trapping the loose end to form the knot. When satisfied that the knot is correct, pull on the line again to make the knot slide up the hook shank. I like to do one last thing—to pull, with equal pressure, on both lines to effectively seat the knot. Pressure from a strong fish will make the spade-end whipping knot draw even tighter.

Knots for joining lines
I do not recommend joining lines unless there is a definite purpose. On a coarse fishing reel a broken line is best discarded and destroyed. Joining a line that has broken a few yards or metres in from the end will be a constant source of trouble in casting and at the same time create a

Double-blood knot

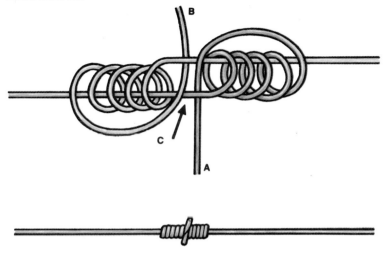

weakness. Better to work farther down on the spool until you are able to replace the nylon, bringing it back up to the correct height on the spool. However, if a line *has* to be joined there is a correct knot that is intended to join lines of similar thickness. It's the double-blood knot. To tie it, lay the ends of nylon alongside one another with an overlap of at least 10 in (25 cm). *It is a false economy to attempt to tie any knot and be miserly with nylon. Nylon is cheap and the break has produced drawn out-ends that are always a source of weakness.* Twist line A over line B to make four coils. Then take the free end and pass it through between the lines at point C. Do the same with line B bringing the free end through point C from the reverse side. Lick the nylon and pull both standing lines equally until the knot pulls up with all coils neatly bedded down.

There are two other line-to-line joining knots. The water knot appears in the fly fishing section as it is used to form droppers on a fly cast. Droppers are not needed by the coarse fisherman. The casting leader knot, used by sea anglers fishing from the shore, is intended for joining two lines of vastly different thickness.

A knot for joining line to your spool

Whether fixed-spool or multiplier, your reel line must be securely tied on. This knot will not slip around the core of the spool. Tie a secure stop knot on the free end of the nylon or braided line. Trim off the scrap before pulling the knot up, for it is very difficult to do this after tightening.

A knot for joining hook lengths to the reel line.

Many anglers prefer to use hooks already tied to known lengths of nylon. For convenience sake, the manufacturer provides an overhand loop on the hook to nylon. This requires a similar knot to be tied into the reel line by the angler. Take the end of the reel line and double it back for 3 in (7.5 cm) or so. Form a loop in the doubled line. Pinch the loop between thumb and fore-finger. Then pass the open loop around the trapped double loop in a complete circle. Finish by passing the open loop through the centre of the double loop. Lubricate and pull up the overhand loop. (Sometimes this knot is called the figure-of-eight knot.)

The reel line and hook length can be easily joined by passing the hook through the reel line loop and then back through its own loop. Trim off all excess nylon from the knots to prevent mid-air tangles. Make sure the knot is tight, otherwise a short end may come disastrously adrift.

A sliding float stop knot

There are two variants of stop knot that each have their use when fishing a sliding float technique. The choice depends very much on the thickness of nylon in use and possibly the size of the rod rings through which the stop knot has to travel. For fine tackle fishing, either using sliding float in stillwater or even when fishing over rod length in a deep river, I would use a wisp of nylon coiled around the reel line as in the illustration. The value of this knot is that it can be moved by finger pressure when required although it rarely moves under float pressure. Pike fishing often requires the use of quite a substantial float. The reel line is reasonably thick—12–15 lb (5–7 kg) b.s. isn't unrealistic— and the stepped-up rod will have fairly large open rings. So, we can use a simple clove-hitch to hold a slip of rubber band. The rubber band should be flexible enough to glide through the rings but has sufficient substance to stop the line running through the plastic tube with which most pike floats are fitted. One other reason for using the band and an easily tied knot is that piking weather often means cold fingers that refuse to cooperate with the stop knot in nylon!

Line-to-spool knot

tie off end
of line with
a half-hitch

Overhand loop knot

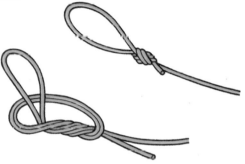

Sliding stop knot

reel line

leave ⅛ in/3 mm tags

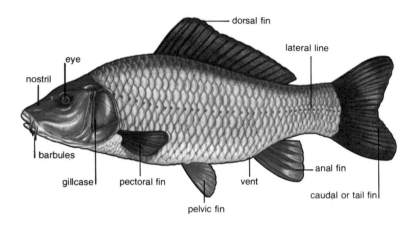

dorsal fin

lateral line

eye

nostril

barbules

gillcase

pectoral fin

vent

anal fin

caudal or tail fin

pelvic fin

(Above) *The river carp, showing the external identification features common to most freshwater fishes.*
(Right) *A superb rudd/bream hybrid caught by Trevor King fishing the Grand Canal at Sallins, Co Kildare, Eire.*
(Below) *The powerful, bottom-hugging barbel, a fish that never gives up.*

COARSE FISH SPECIES

Geographical location, type of river or stillwater, temperature range—all are factors that aid our identification of fish habitat. So, as anglers, we can with some certainty say that a particular area will have defined species. Now we set about our fishing and the moment of truth emerges. Having caught a fish, can we identify it with accuracy?

There are, too, clear identifying features about each separate species—shape of body, size, position and number of fins. Lastly, there is coloration, although this can alter considerably from juvenile to mature fish and even vary between sexes, but not as much as one finds in birds. You will notice that I have not mentioned size as being a necessary identifying key, for it is nowhere as accurate as would be expected among mammals and birds. Fish grow throughout their lifetime and in size vary tremendously from water to water.

There are a number of species, in fresh and saltwater, that only a scientist, specializing in fish, could identify immediately, because fish do play games with Mother Nature! They mate with fish of another species, producing hybrids that look something like both parents. Sometimes man, in his attempt to breed faster growing food fish (carp are farmed commercially on the Continent), comes up with fish that have altered colouring, scale growth or body shape. There are also quirks of nature in fish that lack the species colour or are the 'wrong way round'—as can often be seen in flounders—but this is confined to some marine species.

This is a handbook about the sport of freshwater fishing, for those fish that are of interest to anglers. So I've left out some of the lesser fish, those that are either too small or too rare to mention at length. The burbot is one species that people talk about but I have yet to meet anyone who has caught one or even been present at a capture.

Barbel *Barbus barbus*

A powerful adversary that is found in a number of large rivers and their feeder streams. The barbel is widespread in southern Europe. It was formerly confined to the South and East of England but was introduced into rivers of the West Midlands some years ago. The species likes clean water, high in oxygen content, which means reasonably free from pollution. Just looking at the barbel will tell you where it swims. A long, streamlined shape, driven by strong fins and a large tail—all of which says fast-flowing streams

The barbel has a rounded back yet has a flattened belly. So we might be correct in thinking that the fish feeds on the bottom where it can hug the ground while the current passes swiftly over the fish's back. This view is backed up by a look at the mouth. There are four fleshy appendages, called barbules, spaced around the fish's jaw. They are organs of detection, finding food perhaps in a rushing stream in total darkness. Barbel have an amazing mouth, it is like a tube that can be extended down into the gravel and mud to seek out the invertebrate life that forms the fish's diet.

Angling for barbel means finding suitable swims that will hold the feeding fish. Clean, deepish water over a gravel bottom with growths of streamer weed are good places. The weed will house a myriad of water insects, all of which have an aquatic larval stage in their growth forming a constant supply of food to waiting fish. Anglers should try maggot, worms and meat hookbaits as a first choice. Bread, cheese and natural baits, such as hempseed, will also lure the species.

If there is one thing barbel fishing demands it is groundbait, and plenty of it. Whatever the fishing style, which can be from trotting to static legering, a constant supply of morsels ought to be fed into the head of the swim. Barbel are shoal fish and have huge appetites. So get some feed into the water. When trotting, the loose feed can be thrown in by hand but legering means that the groundbait has to be got down fast to where the baited hook is going to lie. So a swimfeeder becomes a necessary part of the tackle make-up. If a swim has a lot of streamer weed, I prefer to use a rolling leger technique. On a small stream the loose feed can be thrown out, though maggots or worms will have to be given some weight to get them out across the water and then down to the river bed. A heavy cereal groundbait, with hook samples added to the mixture, is far easier to throw. When legering on a big river, the catapult comes in handy to 'fire' the feed with some degree of accuracy.

(Left) *Maggots escape, one after the other, from a swimfeeder to keep a constant stream of food particles trickling through the swim.* (Right) *Here is a nice swim for barbel. The deep glide has a steady current that brings food downstream, or from the swimfeeder, to the fish that lie under rocks causing the turbulence on the surface.*

(Above) *A trio of perfectly scaled barbel from the Severn, a river that holds a good head of this species.* (Right) *Luncheon meat is a fine barbel bait but it does not cast well, easily pulling off the hook. Prevent this by inserting a wisp of grass inside the hookbend before pulling the barb of the hook into the centre of the luncheon meat.*

Specimen hunter Allen Edwards firing maggots from his catapult. The distance and accuracy over hand throwing is astonishing.

On some rivers there can be little choice of bait as fish have been bombarded with but one. There was a time when barbel in the Royalty Fishery, on the Hampshire Avon, would only take maggot baits. They had become 'educated' by the hundreds of fishermen who fed gallons of maggots into the water each week. On the River Severn, barbel have become a normal part of an angler's bag. They appear regularly among the catch of matchmen who throng the banks during the season.

Tackle for barbel fishing must be strong, for both fish and conditions are powerful. I'm aware that many barbel are handled on match rods and quite successfully so, but in pleasure fishing one always assumes that we are going to contact good-sized specimens!

There are two rods suitable for the basic barbel fishing styles; a long-trotting float rod of 11–12 ft (3–3.5 m), giving maximum control of both float and hooked fish, and a traditional leger rod, something like Richard Walker's Mark 4 Avon. Both have the strength and hooking power, at distance, that barbel demand. Today, there are many rods that fall into the same category of length, purpose and power.

Reels are simple to suggest—use whatever suits you best. I like a

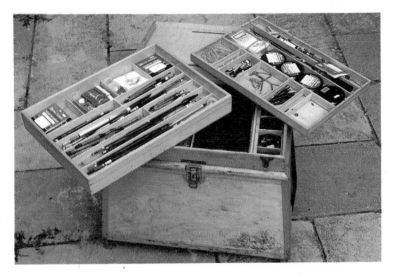

Most anglers' boxes are both a seat and a container for all the accessories they accumulate, held in neat and tidy compartments.

centrepin for trotting. It gives that positiveness of control so necessary when trotting down in an uninterrupted fashion. Control of the fighting fish is in the hands of the angler, not via the mechanics of a slipping drag system that can smother much of the scintillating moments of the tussle. Trotting doesn't call for free-casting ability in the reel, so it's a rare angling treat to be able to fish a situation that is made for the reel. The fixed-spool, whether open or closed-faced, has become the reel for most coarse fishing applications. Certainly, legering for barbel is suited because of the accuracy of putting a bait down into the water just where you want it. Both reels should be loaded with a minimum line strength of 5 lb (2 kg) b.s., though in heavy water even that would be a little on the light side. More often than not, barbel have to be held hard. This means that every part of the tackle set-up must be precisely balanced and no weak areas tolerated. Tie hooks direct to the main line, or, when legering, use a quality link between hook length and reel line. A round bend, forged hook is demanded, of size 8–12 depending on the quality of barbel that you have in your own water. Keep the knots few in number, the tucked half-blood (page 49) is the only one necessary in either rig.

An Avon trotting rig for medium water conditions and an upstream wind. The float is trotted at the speed of the current, then checked momentarily to ensure that the hookbait precedes the float through the swim. Check the float position so the bait travels just off the bottom. The Avon float will cope with swims up to about ⅘ths of the rod length in depth. (Inset) The fluted Avon float combats strong upstream winds and the turbulent currents that spoil good control of the rig.

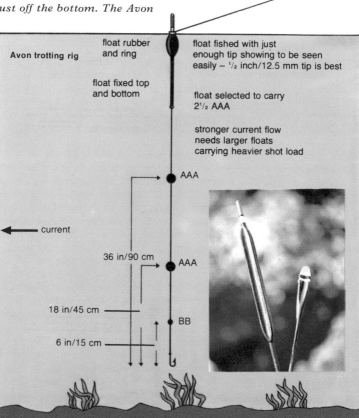

Avon trotting rig

float rubber and ring

float fixed top and bottom

float fished with just enough tip showing to be seen easily – ¹/₂ inch/12.5 mm tip is best

float selected to carry 2¹/₂ AAA

stronger current flow needs larger floats carrying heavier shot load

AAA

← current

36 in/90 cm

AAA

18 in/45 cm

BB

6 in/15 cm

Floats for trotting down a sizeable bait need to have substance in the body. The Avon model will give control, bait and shot carrying capacity. You will also find that plenty of lead is needed to get the bait down fast through the water. Barbel feed tight on the river bed, with their heads down, so there is little point in a light float that skims the bait downstream clear of their heads. In light-flowing streams, where there isn't the pull and urgency of flow, small baits would be perfectly well presented using a balsa stick float. Conditions that produce a strong upstream wind call for a float that 'bites' into the water, and the fluted Avon is a perfect instrument to beat the surface breeze.

Why float fish at all, you might well think, if wind and water conditions are against it being a practical technique? Surely legering would overcome most of the difficulties. That may be so but float fishers get a satisfaction of beating those conditions which form part of their day. If adapting their habitual style then results in a few fish, so much the better. For isn't that what fishing is all about—personal pleasure?

A word about landing nets and keepnets. In the angling Press and elsewhere, the barbel has been the subject of much discussion in relation to the type of netting that should or should not be allowed. Without doubt barbel are at risk with certain forms of net. The problem is that the barbel has a ray, the longest in the dorsal fin, that is a stiff spine with a serrated rear edge and this becomes entangled in the mesh of keepnets. The inevitable twisting of the fish's body results in damage to the fin. Ideally, barbel should not be kept in nets. However, when buying a keepnet, go for the largest that you can afford. Get minnow or gudgeon (a soft knitted mesh) and make certain that the support rings really will keep the net expanded under strong flow conditions. A 10 ft (3 m) net, with a diameter of 18–24 in (45–60 cm), will give the fish room to turn round easily without snagging fins or gill covers.

Trotting floats need to be made in a range of sizes and shot-carrying capacities to cope with fishing conditions of changing current and wind strength. It is a good idea always to mark your floats with their correct shot-loadings. This can be done at home and saves a great deal of time at the waterside prior to fishing.

Bleak *Alburnus alburnus*

One of the smaller species that is of little angling importance other than to be occasionally used as a livebait when perch and pike fishing. The bleak is a silvery fish, with a green tinge to the back. It swims in large shoals in rivers and streams, sometimes in lakes, out in open water. Bleak like clear water and do not often venture into muddy conditions. They feed on minute insect larvae, midges and gnats, but will take a single maggot. When float fishing for other, larger species, anglers often have to use heavy shot loadings to get down, quickly through the bleak shoal.

Common or bronze bream *Abramis brama*

There is a saying that big waters produce big fish. And this is undoubtedly true of the common bream. The species grows best in stillwaters, although there are a number of river systems that have shoals of huge fish. The bream is distributed throughout England and Ireland though there are few waters in Wales with a significant head of fish. Only the Lowlands of Scotland contain bream lakes that produce regular catches. The species is well represented in European lakes and rivers, even though the fish has to compete with many other close relatives within the genus.

Nobody could fail to identify the adult common bream. It is a deep-bodied, laterally compressed fish. Small in the head, bream develop a pronounced hump that leads up to the sharply pointed dorsal fin. The tail is deeply forked and appears rather large for the size of the fish's body.

Juvenile common bream are sometimes mistaken for adult specimens of another bream, the silver *Blicca bjoerkna* which is, at a casual glance,

Bleak

Bream

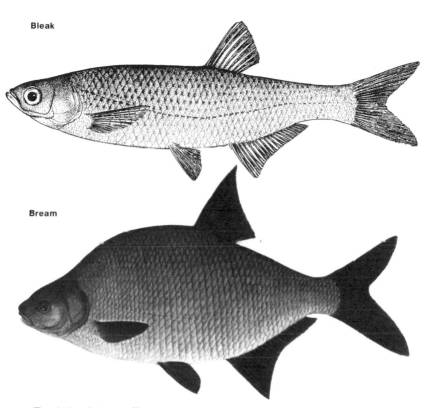

(Far left) *A large-diameter keepnet lets big fish turn round without snagging fins or losing scales. When possible, do not retain large specimens in keepnets. Note their weight and release them.* (Left) *Silver bream have big eyes and their pectoral fins show a reddish tinge.* (Right) *Dennis Burgess with a very satisfactory bag of good bream and rudd.*

almost identical to the larger bronze species. The problem is that the common bream is silvery-white for the first years of its life after which it becomes a deep, brown-black on the back and sides of the body, with a pale cream-yellow tinge to the belly. The silver bream retains this colouring through its life. Scale count and an examination of the branched anal fin rays are the sure way to differentiate between the common and silver breams. Scientists also compare the pharyngeal or throat teeth, but it is necessary to kill the fish to identify it in this way.

Common bream: Scales along the lateral line	51–60
Anal fin branched rays	24–28
Silver bream: Scales along the lateral line	40–55
Anal fin branched rays	20–26

Spawning takes place in May and June, depending upon geographical location. The huge shoals tend to break down into smaller breeding groups, one male fish trying to attract a number of gravid females to its established spawning territory. The male fish exhibit a flush of warty growths on the head, gillcases and forward section of the body. These tubercles disappear soon after the breeding is over.

Spawning is a sight to behold. Bream splash noisily in among the shallow, reeded margins, disturbing the mud and silt and raising great clouds that colour the surrounding water. Bream produce an enormous number of eggs. Hundreds of thousands are extruded to stick on the leaves and stalks of waterplants where they hatch in about a week, if the temperature is high enough. Growth in the common bream depends on the quality of the available food in any water. Some of the Irish lakes have a remarkable ability to produce bream of huge size in a relatively few years. On average, a common bream will take ten years to reach maturity, when it would weigh anywhere between $1\frac{1}{2}$ and 5 lb (0.5–2 kg) but much depends on food supply and quality.

Bream are grazing fish, they move, head down, in a shoal that proceeds across the bed of any water eating almost anything that comes into their path. Most small creatures, such as mussels, worms, midge larvae and emergent ephemerid flies will be eagerly eaten. To catch bream successfully, whether in running or stillwater situations, we have to observe three rules:

1. Find and recognize the feeding bream shoal.
2. Put in groundbait that the shoal can move onto.
3. Hold the fish within the effective fishing area by feeding them continuously.

(Top) *The luxuriant weed growth above a muddy bottom of land drainage canals makes a perfect bream habitat. They feed on the small waterlife that lives in these conditions.* (Left) *In the breeding season male bream show white spawning tubercles.* (Below) *One of the author's favourite bream swims in Bridget Lake, Co Clare, Eire.*

As bream feed, they create a disturbance as they root among the bottom-growing weeds and in the mud, searching out the minute creatures that form their natural diet. In doing this the fish perform a suck-blow operation that releases gas which ascends to the water's surface as a cloud of minute bubbles. This activity provides us with a clue about the fish's whereabouts. Obviously our groundbaiting tactics must be to lay a patch of feed in a situation where we have perfect fishing access to the shoal. It would be pointless to put groundbait into an area where we could not fish efficiently.

Sometimes you will be fortunate to witness the shoal travel toward and move onto your feed. But, at other times it will be the first movement of the float or swingtip that indicates the arrival of bream. Having got the fish, with their heads down on the feed, we have to keep them there. This is best done by continually putting in small amounts of loose feed in order that the interest of the shoal can be sustained. It would be a mistake to bombard the fish with more groundbait as bream can be flighty. Although there are times when nothing seems to scare the shoal away from the carpet of groundbait on which they have begun to feed!

I must admit to preferring a float-fishing approach when breaming. I find that on a stillwater the perpendicular line from float to hook is less likely to give so many line bites. The problem, when fishing for bream, is that there can be a great deal of movement among the fish that form the shoal. They are continuously flashing to and fro striking the line. All bream anglers have had the false bite that showed as a streamer of bream slime on the hook length, although the bait went untouched.

I tend to fish fairly fine, providing the water is relatively clear of obstructions or heavy weed patches. A 12 ft (3.5 m) rod balanced to $3\frac{1}{2}$ lb (1.5 kg) b.s. with the line taken straight through to the hook. It helps to know something about the water and its bream potential before the decision about tackle is made. On a water known for big fish I would probably go up to a b.s. of 5 or 6 lb (2.5 kg). But heavier lines, with larger hooks, do not necessarily put fish off. Once a bream shoal has got down to feeding, they tend to remain until the food supply has been exhausted.

One thing will put bream off the feed and that is for a hooked fish to be allowed free rein by the angler. Any fish that tears through the swim will quickly frighten the shoal. A hooked bream has to be struck, then guided away from the remaining shoal members.

Any bream shoal containing extra large specimens will be particularly scary. After a fright, the shoal will rapidly disperse and it will be some time before they regroup to begin feeding once more. Smaller bream, skimmers as they are often called, will not be quite so easily frightened.

Legering for bream

It has been my experience that really large common bream will not venture too close in to the margins of a lake. In stillwater they seem to keep a healthy 20 yd (18 m) or so out from an angler's pitch.

Many lakes have water of over rod depth which means that you either have to adopt sliding float methods or be prepared to use a legering technique. If the bed of a bream lake is excessively weedy I go for the running leger method illustrated in which the lead weight precedes the hookbait. Advantages in its use are many. The hook will lie on the top of a layer of thick weed even though the casting lead may well be deep within the waterplants. Use a nylon link between the sinker and its connection to the main line of sufficient length to ensure free-running when a fish takes the baited hook. I stop the running link, a Mustad split ring, by pinching on a No. 6 split shot, although a leger stop device would serve equally well.

Big fish mean the use of big baits, so up we go in hook size to something around size 8 or 10 for lobworms. A pinch of flake is best mounted on a size 6. But do not economize when purchasing hooks for heavy bream fishing. Buy the best forged, short-shank hook available,

Link leger with leger stop

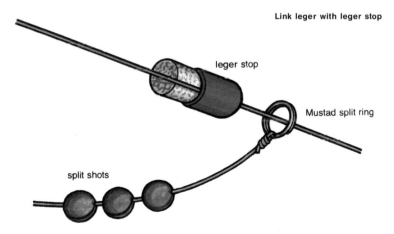

An easily formed link leger rig, using a leger stop to adjust the trace length. Split shots are mounted on a nylon link tied to a free-sliding split-link. A simple, effective leger set-up.

Hooking a lobworm

(Left) *A lobworm should be hooked twice. It lessens the chance of a bream biting the worm off.* (Right) *This butt indicator gives visual and audible signal of a bream run. Easily detached, it is fitted with a snapcatch ring.* (Below) *John Woods holds a heavy bream on his swingtip rod and is playing the fish out in deepwater before netting it in the extremely shallow margins of the lake.*

then, before tying it to the rig, check the barb and point. When fishing over long distances, 20 yd (18 m) or more, it is particularly difficult to set the hook in the gristly jaw of a large common bream, so we need the services of a rod with power in the blank. Although leger rods are becoming shorter, I still advocate the use of something around 10 ft (3 m). A rod with plenty of action right through to the butt, capable of balancing to lines of 4–6 lb (2–2.5 kg) gives a degree of control over casting and playing fish that the shorter rod lacks. I also avoid the fast-tapered rod, favoured by the matchman. Its reaction to a strike *is* fast but this can cause a line break when the power of the strike is met by the solid resistance of a weighty slab-sided bream.

Bites from bream, however big, vary enormously and detecting them is difficult. I've had fish that almost tore the swingtip from the rod and yet, when fishing the Grand Canal in Ireland, medium-sized fish have given the merest $\frac{1}{8}$ in (3 mm) lift on the swingtip. I think that the type of bite varies according to the need for the fish to feed and the amount of competition present. Small fish, living in a large shoal, tend to feed more readily, grabbing food where they can. The larger, specimen-sized fish are far more wary of the hookbait.

It is often said that the best bream fishing takes place in the darker hours, either early morning or late into the evening. Certainly, I have had experiences that give credit to the theory. But bite detection becomes a problem in low light conditions. At such times I prefer to use a butt indicator. Poised near to the rod handle, it is more easily seen to move and a powerful run will snap the indicator against the rod making a definite noise. Of course, the bobbin can be a relatively simple affair. One can pinch on a piece of dough or attach a cork float to be seen in the halflight. Probably the most effective butt indicator, from a clear vision aspect, is a modern glow bobbin.

Silver bream *Blicca bjoerkna*
Silver bream are found in the British Isles only in the rivers and lakes of East Anglia and the fenlands where they rarely attain a body weight of more than 1 lb (0.5 kg). On the Continent of Europe, however, *Blicca* is said to grow to 2–3 lb (1–1.5 kg) and be more widely distributed among the rivers, canals and stillwaters. Silver bream closely resemble immature common bream for which they are often mistaken. Though similar in shape, the silver species has a much slimmer body shape. The eye is

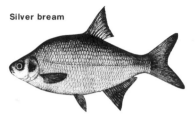
Silver bream

(Right) *Three bream species from Holland; common and silver bream and schneider. The red fins belong to a rudd.*

considerably larger in proportion to the size of the fish and there is a pronounced snub nose. Both pelvic and pectoral fins display a reddish tinge with a dark tip coloration. The fish's body is covered in silver-white scales that are easily removed if the bream is roughly handled.

The species is not deliberately fished for but is often found in the keepnets of anglers fishing in the East of England. Techniques are similar to those used for roach, common bream and other river species.

Carp *Cyprinus carpio*

Carp are distributed throughout Europe. They were brought there and into the British Isles from Asia. Within Britain the carp is confined to England, with a number of discreet locations in Wales and the Lowlands of Scotland. Carp have been introduced into Ireland, where they are confined to small waters in County Cork. The Inland Fisheries Trust of Ireland are, at this time, developing a breeding programme for the dispersal of carp to a number of coarse fishing waters.

There is only one species of true carp in Britain, although there are three distinct varieties. Carp are easily identified. They are deep-bodied, heavily-built fish, possessing a long dorsal fin. Around the mouth there are four barbules: two long appendages growing from the corner of the fish's mouth, with two smaller barbules sprouting from above the top lip. The common carp is a completely scaled fish, dark purple scaling on the back shades to orange flanks which soften into a brilliant cream on the belly.

Mirror carp have similar coloration but have only a few large scales, generally to be found along the lateral line. The leather variety has no scales and is often of a softer, paler colour.

The common carp also has a habitat variation, the river carp, which is a sleeker fish that has adapted to living in the streamy water of some European rivers. Unlike its stillwater cousins, the river carp does not attain the huge size that anglers come to expect of this species. No doubt this is due to the expenditure of much energy to combat the currents. The carp is burning food that would otherwise have gone to build tissue.

Carp spawn in the warm months of May and June. It is a vigorous exercise, frequently witnessed by English anglers out inspecting water during their close season. The fish move into extremely shallow water, among beds of dense waterweed, where they splash and chase noisily while expelling the eggs and fertilizing milt. Carp have been bred for centuries by man for food, and because of this the 'manufactured' varieties seem to have difficulties when the spring weather is unduly cold. Female fish can spawn hundred of thousands of eggs, each about a millimeter in diameter. The eggs, slightly sticky, attach to the fronds of waterplants where they hatch in about one week, depending on the ambient temperature.

Carp love muddy, deep water with a lush growth of weed. Their diet

The best waters for big carp are those with a prolific weed growth.

is composed of minute water creatures. It is claimed that they also derive a part of their food from algae and other vegetation. This feeding behaviour makes the carp a difficult fish to encourage to feed on the angler's baits. We cannot put the microscopic food onto a hook and so there is an element of education on the part of carp anglers. They gradually introduce the species to accept larger baits that can be used on a sensible size hook.

Carp react to calculated groundbaiting techniques. They are not shoal fish in the sense that they congregate in large feeding groups. It is necessary to bait particular swims in a pattern that encourages the carp to develop a habit of feeding in a place chosen by the angler. Carp can be difficult fish to handle; hooking and playing needs to be in a situation where the angler can beat the fish in reasonably open water. Snaggy, tench-like swims may look inviting but they allow this powerful fish to fight on its own terms. Carp are notorious for diving into lilypads and other places from where they cannot be withdrawn on other than excessively strong lines.

Carp are one of the few coarse species that feed at all depths. Fishermen can adopt a wide variety of techniques to catch them, even though the species has a reputation for becoming 'educated' when a particular method is over-used.

It is almost impossible to make hard and fast recommendations for suitable rods to beat carp as a species. The fish can vary tremendously in body weight from water to water. I regularly fish a lake where there are hundreds of small carp, fish of 1–5 lb (0.5–2 kg) but nothing larger. Such specimens can be played easily on a 12 ft (3.5 m) match rod. On the other hand, there are many waters in Europe where the fish reach an average weight of over 20 lb (9 kg), with a number of individuals scaling over 40 lb (18 kg). Such large carp need the stopping power of specialized leger rods that can cast a bait weighing an ounce (28 g) yet land a fish of mighty proportions and fighting ability!

(Left) *Artery forceps are the best disgorgers for the leathery mouthed fish.* (Right) *Strange bedfellows! A common carp and a chub both from the River Trent. The carp has found a warm, slow-running area, while the chub prefers cooler, livelier and well oxygenated water.*

Average carp can be handled adequately on a 10 ft (3 m) leger rod, designed to have a test curve of 1 lb (0.5 kg), balanced to a line of around 6 lb (2.5 kg) b.s. Larger carp call for a *stepped-up* rod that mates with lines of 10–14 lb (4.5–6 kg). The fishing may involve casting baits over long distances, so rods must have the punch to get a bait away. Often no lead is used on the terminal rig, the weight of the bait being sufficient to carry the rig out. With rods of such varied casting weight and fish sizes, it is not surprising that carp rods have evolved as distinct weapons having little or no similarity to rods used habitually on the other freshwater species. If a carp rod can be asked to perform another function, it is as a salmon spinner where the power of quarry and weight of bait are again widely separated.

Fixed-spool reels are universally used for carp fishing. Anglers should buy those that have stout gearing, a roller incorporated in the bale arm assembly and a slipping drag system that can be finally adjusted to cope with the immense and protracted fight that carp can give. Always load the spool to its correct, frictionless, position with at least 200 yd (180 m) of nylon line. It is also a shrewd practice to change the line after each fishing season. Nylon lines lose their strength in time and are very cheap to replace.

Surface fishing
One of the most delightful carp fishing methods is to lure fish to a bait that floats on the surface. Breadcrust is the bait, cast out on a weightless rig to lie alongside reedbanks and other cover that may hide carp. The forged hook is tied direct to the reel line and enough casting weight is gained by dipping the crust momentarily into the water. It picks up sufficient added weight to ease the flow of line through the rod rings. A drawback to the use of a floating bait is that it is at the mercy of wind and surface drift. Some anglers advise laying the line over lilypads to tether the crust but I don't like the method. It places drag on the bait when taken by a feeding fish, which may cause the carp to spit the bait out

This is one of the classic methods for stillwater carp fishing. A floating crust can be tethered in a fixed fishing position with this rig. Adjust the sinker nylon link length to keep the split ring clear of the thick weed that can rise from the lakebed.

Carp fishing: floating crust

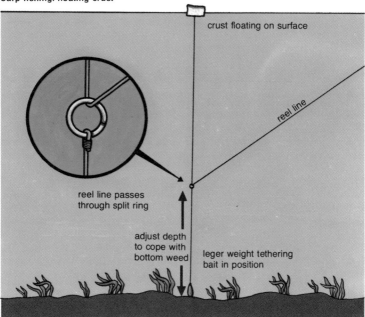

crust floating on surface

reel line

reel line passes
through split ring

adjust depth
to cope with
bottom weed

leger weight tethering
bait in position

Balanced crust

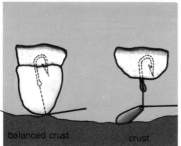

balanced crust

crust

Potato and crust

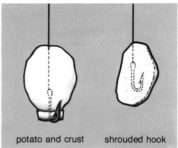

potato and crust

shrouded hook

74

before a hooking chance occurs. Another fault of the method is that the line could snag in the tough lily stalks.

I don't find a drifting bait wrong as a presentation method. After all, carp are conditioned to expect feed drifting on the surface naturally as it drops from trees and bankside vegetation.

Fishing for carp is a waiting game. The pitch has to be set out in a logical order with every part of the tackle set up ready to hand. I suppose the most used angling system is to have a leger rod, on two rests, poised at the angle that the line enters the water. After the cast is made the bale arm is left open with a loop of line hanging down on which a visible indicator hangs. This can be as simple as a piece of silver paper. If a fish takes the bait there will be an immediate response from the indicator. It will lift slowly or jump into the air, depending on the take.

The rod is taken in the hand but the reel retrieve is not engaged. We wait for a run to develop. The line will often peel off the spool and then stop. This is the time to close the bale arm because the fish has stopped its flight. Now we have the dilemma of whether to wait for a further movement from the fish or to quickly wind in to regain perfect contact with the carp. There can be no hard and fast rule, for fish behave differently from day to day. I prefer to recover line smoothly until I am assured that there is little slack left between the rod tip and fish. The drag setting on the reel should be set before you begin fishing.

Striking must be a positive sweep-back of the rod. Keep the rod tip high until a definite fighting pressure is felt. This has the effect of making certain that the hook is set into the carp, for often, with a lot of line out, there is difficulty in setting a stout hook. A tight line will ensure that the fish pulls the hook home. Keeping the rod up gives an immediate indication of what the fish is doing. One feels the first rushes and can absorb these first movements with the spring of a compressed rod. An important tip: never point the rod at a powerful, running fish.

(Far left) *Legered bread can sink into weed, so balance it with a pasteball. A leger weight will not be needed. When fishing a hard-bottomed lake, a crust is cast with a leger bomb but the natural buoyancy in the crust will lift it above the bottom weed, where it can be seen by feeding fish.*

(Left) *Thread a potato onto the hook with a needle. It will fly off if cast vigorously, so a piece of crust or grass (see page 57) will hold it on the hook. Do not make paste too stodgy, and form the bait by flattening it round the hook so that it will lay flat on the bottom instead of sinking into the ooze.*

Crucian carp *Carassius carassius*

Crucian carp are fish of the small ponds and lowly waters. They thrive where other, larger members of the carp family would have difficulty in finding enough food and oxygen to support life. Overgrown habitats, laced with thick waterweed, will provide the crucian with a plentiful food supply where other fish would starve. There are very few areas of Western Europe that do not have this species. The fish were introduced both as food and as an ornamental species, rather like the goldfish, which is a close relative.

The crucian carp is easily identified as a stumpy, deep-bodied fully-scaled fish lacking the barbules found on its larger relatives. It has a protracted spawning period, often exhibiting several distinct egg producing periods. The eggs, over 200,000 in number, stick to underwater vegetation and hatch in about a week if the temperature is above 66°F (19°C). Man has produced a hybrid between the crucian and common carp. In Eastern Europe, these hybrids are used as a food fish that will grow to table weights in a relatively short time. Because the fish are sterile, they do not expend energy in sexual behaviour.

Crucian carp feed on minute animal life, the seeds of plants and the larvae of many of the insects that inhabit stillwaters. This feeding behaviour determines what anglers can usefully employ as hookbaits.

Tackling up for crucian carp fishing presents no difficulty. They aren't big fish, so a standard float-fishing outfit will be adequate. The accent must be on fine lines, floats and small hooks capable of a delicate approach to this gentle species. The crucian can be attracted by cloud

(Right) *This is a standard light stillwater float rig for when fishing a rod-length or so out onto a calm surface. Fished near the bottom, the bait will sink slowly due to the shot pattern. The float will sit upright with the large shot, then the lower shots sink before settling the float deeper. Then the bottom shots add their weight to the delicate float. Bird quills vary in size, so buy several to experiment with their loading capacity. The larger quills will allow you to fish the slowest rivers while retaining a perfect sensitivity.* (Below) *Groundbait for crucian carp needs to be soft and crumbly. Adding a few maggots, as a hookbait sample, is a good idea. Do not overdo groundbaiting, one needs to attract fish – not feed them! Small knobs of feed that break into a cloud of loose particles will bring crucian carp to the immediate area of the hookbait.*

Sensitive rig for stillwater

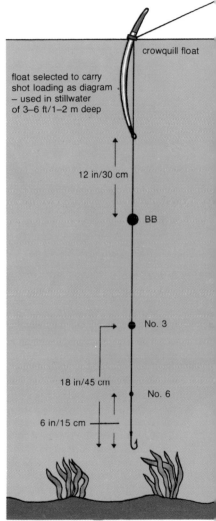

crowquill float

float selected to carry shot loading as diagram – used in stillwater of 3–6 ft/1–2 m deep

12 in/30 cm

BB

No. 3

18 in/45 cm

No. 6

6 in/15 cm

baiting the chosen fishing area. Mix a light, crumbly groundbait that will sink gradually through the water with telling effect. Do not throw in large balls of feed that disturb the stillness of the water and provide the crucian with food for a month.

Crucian carp will feed at a variety of depths. So the slow-sinking method and a single maggot or morsel of worm will give good sport particularly when your quarry can see the bait being offered. The fish will leave the cover of thick weed, attracted by sinking particles of cloudbait, move up to the source of food and attack the hookbait. They can put up a fierce struggle for their size and bite well throughout all but the coldest months of the year.

Chub *Leuciscus cephalus*

A fish of the rivers, chub prefer a powerful, steady current that brings both life to the water and food to the fish. This species has two easily recognized indentification features: a big head and mouth and large, silvery scales. The species is extremely widespread and found throughout Europe and into Asia Minor. But the chub are severely restricted within the British Isles. They are found in England and some lowland rivers of Scotland, mainly in the west. The species is all but absent from Wales and is found nowhere in Ireland. There have been some introductions into stillwaters, some of them very successful. It appears that the chub can alter its lifestyle to suit most environments providing there is enough food to satisfy its prodigious appetite.

In the immature stage, the species forms huge shoals, but seems to adopt a solitary mode of living when adult. Chub are slow-growing fish. They mature later than other river fish: males at about four years, with female chub becoming sexually mature at least one year later. The fact that chub are missing from some areas of the British Isles is probably due to their being a very slow-growing fish, full of tiny bones, so not regarded as a species worthy of stocking to form food for humans. A number of our sporting species were introduced on the premise that they could be farmed in some way or other.

Chub seem to be the one species that does spawn within what in England is the legislated close-season. They breed in shallow, clean water, during the months of April-June, where over 100,000 eggs are shed by the gravid females.

This denizen of the dark holes and undercut banks has an omnivorous diet. Practically anything that moves, or drops from above, will be eaten—which is a considerable advantage to the intending chub angler! The fish will rise to take emergent flies, await the falling of each season's wild fruits and seeds, then sink into the depths to search for small creatures and the fry of all fish resident in the river. Chub are greedy and this greed makes them a target for anglers. Rarely will they refuse to feed. Even in times of severe winter cold or flood, the chub can be relied on to provide rod and line sport. They react to plentiful groundbaiting, showing an immediate interest. As soon as a shoal is found and introduced to the groundbait the angler must begin a policy of loose feeding in a ratio to the fish hooked and landed. I throw in a dozen or so

The chub is a fish that will hurl itself at a quietly presented natural or artificial bait. But one 'wrong' movement from the bank will send it down. Chub fishing on the Trent at Holme Pierrepont.

Chub are only one of the river species that respond to a bait that is trotted down to them. This rig, a simple balsa/cane stick float with evenly spaced shots, is fished over-depth on streamy water for any species that abounds. Swing the tackle out, with a slight check on the line to get correct cocking of the float and to let the shot be picked up by the current. Holding the line back smoothly will ensure that the bait goes downstream ahead of the float Frequent checks as the line pulls off will halt the float, causing the bait to rise in the stream. This allows the fish to see the bait and prompts them to investigate.

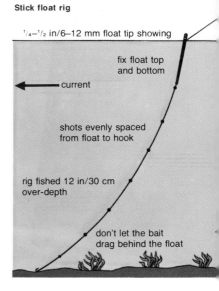

Stick float rig

¹/₄–¹/₂ in/6–12 mm float tip showing

fix float top and bottom

← current

shots evenly spaced from float to hook

rig fished 12 in/30 cm over-depth

don't let the bait drag behind the float

maggots with every cast that I make. This gets the chub used to the hookbait and keeps them moving up towards the baited hook.

Two methods are used when chub fishing; trotting or legering. I must confess to a liking for long-trotting a float down the river. It's all-action angling that keeps one with busy hands and mind. However, there are times and situations where legering is the correct style to effectively fish the swim.

Because chub can be large and powerful fish that use the strong currents to advantage, tackle has to be capable of giving the best sport to the fisherman *and* landing the fish. One has to clearly divide small chub from their larger brethren. The smaller fish that form a large part of the average float-fishing catch can be handled easily on a standard match rod that is balanced to lines of 2–3 lb (1 kg). But where large chub are expected it will take a rod with power to hold and beat the fish. The Avon style rod, formally manufactured from split cane but now available in glass and carbon, has that all-through action so necessary in subduing the protracted fight that a good chub can give. The rod with power and movement through tip to handle can be bent into the fighting curve that tires the specimen. A fixed-spool reel, loaded with 5–7 lb

(2–3 kg) monofilament, completes the standard gear. I find the shorter
10 ft (3 m) Avon well able to handle both legering and trotting methods
with adequate control over the monster if it arrives. I think the modern
swing-tipping rod, often 1 ft (30 cm) or more shorter, just a little too
short for perfect control close into the bank.

Trotting the river is a fishing style that takes the bait down to the bed
of the river, searching out fish over whatever distance the angler feels he
can fish effectively. The usual distance that the float is allowed to travel
is 20–30 yd (18–27 m). Greater distances can never be fished properly,
for the stretch in nylon masks the hook-setting power of the strike,
however exaggerated the sweepback of the rod may be. The secret of
successful trotting is to use a float capable of carrying sufficient shots to
get the bait down quickly to fish and the way in which line is run off the
reel. Ideally, one would use a centrepin reel that provides the ultimate in
line control. Unfortunately, centrepins are no longer freely available in
the tackle shops, so we have to use the fixed-spool. These come in two
kinds; the open-face spool and the closed-face variety.

Trotting from an open-face spool is done by keeping the bale arm open
after the cast and then letting the line peel off the spool while keeping the
index finger hovering over the lip of the spool. The run off and holding
back of the float can be achieved by delicate finger pressure. Problems

(Left) *For chub use casters and a lively white maggot.* (Below left) *An Abu closed-face trotting reel is foolproof in operation.* (Below) *Ideal for trotting too is the skirted spool reel. The bale arm can be flicked shut in a split second to establish contact with a fast-biting fish.*

arise after a strike has been made, for the bale arm has to be closed while pressure is kept on the fish. The new finger closing device, found on skirted reels, helps a lot with this function.

Closed-face reels are more easily controlled when trotting. The pick-up is released and the cast made. Line then flows steadily from the reel. The slightest movement of the reel handle engages the pick-up and contact is made with the fish.

Sharp eyes and good reflexes are the hallmark of the trotting expert. The bite has to be seen; it could be a dipping of the float but might only be an arrested travel, which demands instinctive reaction. Position of the bait, relative to the bed of the stream, is vital. The bait should swim down just clear of the bottom. Obviously, there will be obstructions that

Trotting heavy water in a strong downstream wind rules out stick and Avon floats. You will need a ducker – simply an upsidedown Avon! Like the Avon, the ducker has a good shot-carrying capacity but the buoyancy is underwater where it is less affected by wind. Put half the shots high on the cast, where they sink the line, lock the float depth and instantly cock the float. Do not fish this rig over-depth. The float will travel with the current, so the hook-setting should just clear the riverbed. (Above, far right) The fixed leger is best fished across and down to the chub. Let the weight settle before tightening the line. Fish the rolling leger by casting across the stream and rolling it round to the nearside bank. Lengthening the cast will cover more water. This method works well in winter, when weed has died and the bottom is clear.

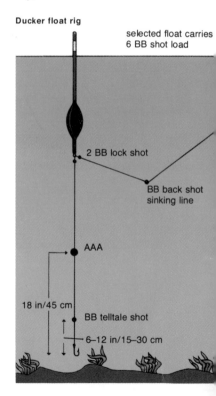

Ducker float rig

selected float carries 6 BB shot load

2 BB lock shot

BB back shot sinking line

AAA

18 in/45 cm

BB telltale shot

6–12 in/15–30 cm

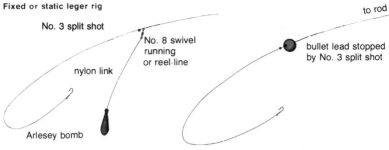

Fixed or static leger rig

No. 3 split shot

No. 8 swivel
running
or reel line

nylon link

to rod

bullet lead stopped
by No. 3 split shot

Arlesey bomb

Rolling leger rig

halt the movement of the bait. Only experience will establish the difference between a momentary hang-up and the attentions of a feeding fish.

It is a sound idea to halt the flow of line at the end of each trot down. This will cause the float to stop, swinging the bait upward. This subtle lift often urges fish to attack. Having made a number of trots, alter the line of float entry to cover fish that may have been watching the bait from off to the side of the float's travel. Having found fish, give them some loose feed to encourage them to move upstream and lose fear of your trotted hookbait.

The decision to adopt a legering style is conditioned by a number of factors: whether the river is too wide to fish with the float, when there are surface obstructions, such as weed, that would severely hamper float fishing and when the weather is very cold. Legering places and holds the bait where it ought to be for efficient angling—hard on the bed of the river. Two variations of the style exist: the static and rolling leger. Their uses differ in that fish must find the bait on the static leger whereas using a rolling technique takes the hookbait in search of the fish.

Fishing the static leger method involves groundbaiting in a defined spot and then casting the baited hook to land within that area. Obviously, accuracy is vital to ensure that one is fishing where the fish can be expected. Chub are a species that demand skill in reading the water. The fish are secretive, they avoid any form of bankside noise, sinking down into the shadows to swim away from the presence of humans. So they have to be stalked.

The leger fisherman can learn a great deal by walking the river. Polarized glasses will enable him to watch the activities of the chub, to identify the lies of big fish and to detect the changes in the river flow when in flood or at times of slackened flow caused by summer drought and water abstraction.

I like to fish unhampered by the traditional coarse fisher's tackle box. Just the made-up rod, with some bait and a single rod rest. Having found a suitable chub lie, the cast is made and the rod supported on the rest. The butt of the rod is held in my right hand and the line taken between the finger and thumb of the left. Touch legering like this is probably the most sensitive method for detecting the bites of any fish when legering. A lot of bites will result in a clear movement on the rod tip. It will either 'bounce' or pull round in a hearty thump to follow the fish. There will be a lot of soft, gently moving bites that are best felt through the direct contact of the line across your fingers. Bites can be reacted to by a sharp, sideways strike that directly opposes the direction of the line.

Fishing the rolling leger presents a slightly different pattern of fishing and style. I dispense with the rod rest, holding the rod throughout the angling session. Casts are made, often from a kneeling position, while trying to remain hidden among the bankside vegetation. I do hold the line but tend to rely more on eyesight for bite detection. I watch the bow in the line between rod tip and where the line enters the water. I strike at any straightening of the line. If the line stops moving progressively, as it follows the rolling lead, a positive strike must be made. It could have been arrested by a fish or blocked by something on the bed of the river but one must react to anything out of the ordinary.

The efficiency of groundbaiting can be increased by adding a through-line swimfeeder to the rig. This type of feeder will roll across a fairly clean bottom without the hang-ups encountered when using blockends of the normal construction.

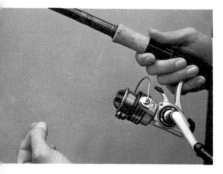
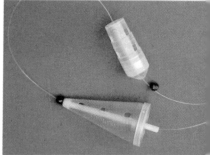

Chub are a species that will rise to a fly and take the nymphs as they rise up to the surface. The fish can be stalked with a fly rod and artificials. A wet-fly rod, floating or sink tip line and a few flies complete the chub man's outfit. With this minimum of tackle and a landing net, one can enjoy a day's fishing that covers an enormous amount of ground. In fact, a day spent walking the bank with a fly rod will enable you to come to know both the species and where the big fish are to be found.

I have most success fishing a team of two nymphs on a 4 lb (2 kg) cast. The tail nymph needs to be slightly leaded, to get down in the stream. The idea is to fish your way upstream, casting into all of the likely holes. The leaded fly will sink down with the mid-cast nymph in the middle level of the stream. Let the cast sink, then strip back the line in jerky, intermittent movements that simulate the action of the natural creature as it rises up to the surface. Let the occasional cast swing round across and downstream. Give the flies life by raising the rod tip, which will draw the nymphs up to the surface. Chub will follow the lures to hit them as they break the surface film.

Chub will also take a dry fly. Traditionally, they take palmered flies, those with a bushy dressing that represent beetles, bees and mothlike insects that fall from the vegetation alongside the river. They are fished

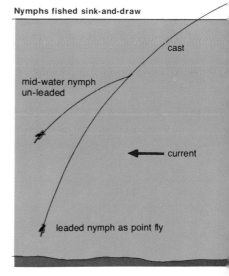

Nymphs fished sink-and-draw

cast

mid-water nymph
un-leaded

current

leaded nymph as point fly

(Far left) *This is easily the most sensitive style of bite detection. The touch legering method depends on lightly holding the reel line between thumb and finger while pointing the rod at the bait, the straight line giving great sensitivity.* (Left) *The line runs right through these swimfeeders.* (Right) *A cast of two nymphs for sink-and-draw fishing to search likely chub holes. The flies are retrieved in a jerky movement, simulating the twitches of live insects as they make their way towards the surface. The nymphs may also attract the attention of feeding trout, for chub and trout often share waterspace.*

as a single fly, cast upstream and allowed to drift down at the speed of the current in a completely natural presentation. Don't fine the nylon cast down below 3 lb (1.5 kg) or thereabouts. Chub are strong fighters and can put up a struggle that will test both tackle and angler.

Dace *Leuciscus leuciscus*

Dace are one of the most widely distributed of our coarse species. Found across the whole of Europe and North Asia are six other, closely related, species that differ little in coloration or average size. Within the British Isles, only the northern parts of Scotland are devoid of this species. Dace are common to rivers and stream, preferring to inhabit stretches of lively flowing water with a high oxygen content.

The species resembles a juvenile chub but more slender in body shape. Both anal and dorsal fins on the dace have concave trailing edges whereas the chub has fins with a pronounced convex rear edge. The eyes of the dace are yellow. During the breeding season, male fish have tubercles that cover the body.

Anal fins of dace and chub

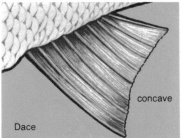

Dace
concave

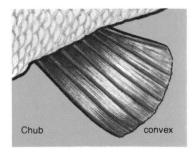

Chub
convex

This silvery fish spends much of its life in the fast-running shallow water, feeding on tiny insects and larvae that emerge from the gravels. They will rise, freely, to suck in creatures that drift down on the fast current. This feeding behaviour enables us to fish for them with trotted natural bait, such as a single maggot, or to present a small dry fly among the tumbling water. Dace aren't big fish but they can provide terrific sport on tackle that lets them show their speed.

Float fishing gives the maximum sport using lightly shotted tackle trotted through the swim. Where conditions dictate I often use the Trent Trotter float devised by the late Billy Lane, who was a master of float fishing technology. His rig, ideal for fishing in shallows where there is little depth over 2 ft (0.5 m) or so, depends on the pendulum effect gained by joining both reel line and hook trail together with the pinched-on split shot. One other factor must be remembered and that is the position of the shot that sinks the reel line. Billy used this rig in water down to 6 in (15 cm) deep, where he found it more effective on the strike, and much less likely to create disturbance to the shoal. The trail is set to fish over depth, add 6 in (15 cm) to the depth of water throughout the swim. The back shot sinks the reel line and is used to lightly trip the bottom, acting as a brake to the tackle as the rig swims downstream.

Dace can be caught in deeper water by standard trotting methods, laying on or even by legering although I much prefer to trot the stream for the satisfaction that fishing at distance can give.

Billy Lane's Trent Trotter Rig

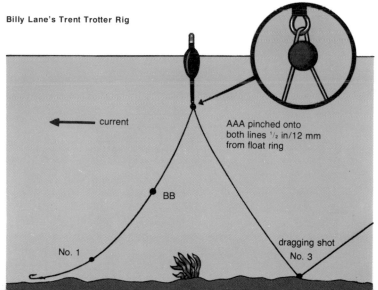

current

AAA pinched onto both lines ½ in/12 mm from float ring

BB

No. 1

dragging shot No. 3

Eel *Anguilla anguilla*

The freshwater eel is an interesting fish. Spawned in the Sargasso Sea far away in the deep western Atlantic, it travels as a minute fish to our shores on a journey that takes three years to complete. During its travels it undergoes a metamorphosis, changing from a flattened, leaflike creature to an elver. Ascending the rivers in millions, these small fish then find their way into practically every form of running and still water.

There is only one species of freshwater eel in European waters. Two colours are known but these are only maturity variations. When actively feeding and growing in fresh and estuarine water, eels adopt a yellow colour. Then, when ready to react to the urge to breed, they become silver, cease feeding and migrate to the sea to begin the passage back to

the eel breeding grounds of the Sargasso Sea. One never finds a 'ripe' eel, for the ovaries and gonads do not develop while the fish is in European waters. Probably, full sexual maturity is achieved only on the migration or when the spawning area is reached.

Eels are both predatory feeders and scavengers. They will eat most other live animals and such dead fish as they find. It is believed that they can exist for long periods without food of any kind.

The freshwater eel is a powerful fish that requires strength in the angler's tackle. Probably the best way to fish for the eel is by legering a bunch of worms or a deadbait laid hard on the bed of a river or lake. These baits may well attract other species, particularly where pike and tench abound. Eels cannot be fished for specifically unless we know that they inhabit the water. In rivers, they are found over the clean bottom of the slow-running stretches. Look for them in the mouths of land drains and smaller waterways that empty into the river. I find that the well-stocked farm pond and small lowland lakes hold good eels. They are a fish that take best after the sun goes down. Though not totally nocturnal in feeding bahaviour, eels favour the dark hours for their wandering over the lake bed in search of dying or dead fish.

(Left) *There are probably eels in every river, stream, pond and drain. Such drains crisscross the Belgian landscape, making splendid eel fisheries. Many of the farmers position nets and plaited reed traps into these waterways, which branch off the main canals. Various kinds of eel trap are also seen in the east of England, where the muddy streams harbour huge numbers of eels.* (Right) *Eel fishing does not call for a cautious and quiet approach from the angler. Eels are usually caught when the sportfisherman is seeking other more sporting quarry. This is a deadbait rig for eel fishing. A bag of oily fish or offal on the swivel helps to attract eels.*

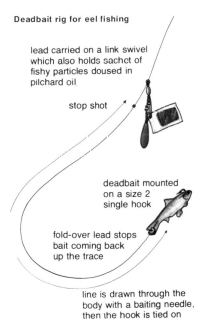

Deadbait rig for eel fishing

lead carried on a link swivel which also holds sachet of fishy particles doused in pilchard oil

stop shot

deadbait mounted on a size 2 single hook

fold-over lead stops bait coming back up the trace

line is drawn through the body with a baiting needle, then the hook is tied on

I admit that I do not fish delicately for the eel. A carp rod and reel loaded with 8 lb (3.5 kg) line is the normal gear. The terminal rig is simple, a No. 2. forged hook tied direct to the reel line with sufficient weight in the lead to carry the bait out and hold it on the bottom. Keep the leger simple by running the lead on the line stopped by a split shot. The addition of a small bag of oily fish (rubby dubby) will help to draw the eel to your hookbait. This can be attached to the casting bomb using a link swivel or, as the well-known writer and tackle innovator Allen Edwards suggests, the bag of offal can be loaded with a stone to provide the weight for casting.

Your problems start after the eel has been hooked. It will writhe and twist constantly, while attempting to wrap itself around sunken branches and other hazards. After the strike is made, the eel must be kept moving. Don't relax the fight for a moment. I do not bother with the landing net. Drag the eel up onto dry land and grab it with a dry cloth. This will allow you to grip the fish, which is incredibly slimy and hard to hold. More often than not the hook cannot be removed, so cut the trace and dump the fish into a sack if you plan to eat it. The fish can be killed after stunning it. A sharp blow with a heavy object across the vent will quieten an eel. Then cut through the flesh and spine behind the head to sever the spinal cord and kill the fish. Hooks can be recovered after the fish is dead.

Grayling *Thymallus thymallus*

The grayling is found throughout Northern Europe and Scandinavia. In Britain, the species is widely distributed in game fish rivers where it vies with trout for the available food. Not everybody regards the grayling as a gamefish, so for this reason I have included the species within the coarse species. Certainly it does not enjoy the protection of the trout close-season but gives many trout anglers the opportunity to extend their sport by fishing late into the autumn for this splendid fighter.

Grayling are a distinctive fish that cause few problems of identification. Possessing an adipose fin, that fleshy appendage between dorsal and tail fins, the species looks like a mullet with an enlarged dorsal fin. The grayling's back is purple, shading to bright, silvery scales with a metallic tinge on the flanks. An uneven pattern of dark spots splash the sides and large dorsal fin of the fish. Unlike the trout, grayling spawn in the spring. Between the months of March and May females construct nests among clean gravel to eject 80,000 eggs or more, which hatch in about a month. The newly-hatched fry feed on minute water creatures. The adults take worms, insects and other small fish.

There are two ways in which to fish for grayling. They will take the artificial fly, but I want to deal with a form of bait fishing that is almost exclusive to the grayling and is a delight to engage in! Trotting a worm down the rough stream on a self-cocking float that bobbles on the tumbling water demands acute eyesight with perfect control of the runningline. I use my 12 ft (3.5 m) match rod, with a fixed-spool reel

Although found in a number of European chalkstreams and trout streams, the grayling is really an Arctic species that prefers highly oxygenated, pollution-free mountain rivers.

loaded with 4 lb (1.5 kg) line. The hook, a size 14 forged, round bend is tied direct. Years ago Reg Righyni, one of the most respected of rod designers, introduced me to his version of the self-cocking balsa float that uses a stainless steel stem to give enough weight to balance the buoyancy of the wood. I have found no reason to alter Reg's float construction after many years of use. The float carries an additional No. 1 shot to get the worm down into the wild water.

Set the float, fixed top and bottom, to trot the worm just over the river bed. The float, which will ride the rough water well, is allowed to swim down with the current but is held back occasionally to swing the worm up from the bottom. This action will give the grayling a clear sight of the bait, encouraging them to take it fearlessly. Don't expect a bite to be shown as a definite pull down of the float! Often the float will halt in its travel as the fish grabs the worm, holding its own position against the

Trotting rig for grayling

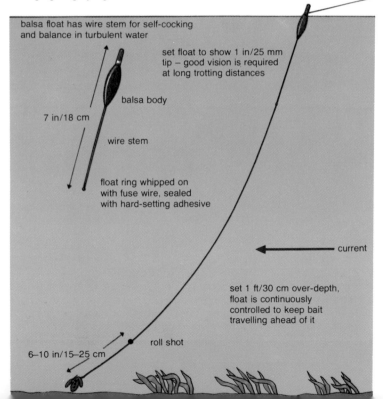

balsa float has wire stem for self-cocking
and balance in turbulent water

set float to show 1 in/25 mm
tip – good vision is required
at long trotting distances

balsa body

7 in/18 cm

wire stem

float ring whipped on
with fuse wire, sealed
with hard-setting adhesive

current

set 1 ft/30 cm over-depth,
float is continuously
controlled to keep bait
travelling ahead of it

roll shot

6–10 in/15–25 cm

current flow. Strike, positively, at any movement that appears out of the ordinary. Remember that you may have a lot of line off the reel. Nylon stretches considerably so the strike must be back over the shoulder to make direct contact with your fish. Grayling have a tough jaw, so a well-set hook will mean a fish in the landing net.

Gudgeon *Gobio gobio*

One of our small fish that anglers will encounter when fishing delicately for roach and other river-dwelling species. The gudgeon is found almost everywhere in Europe. There are many gudgeon species, all of them having two easily seen barbules growing from the corners of the fish's mouth. The gudgeon in British waters lives in running water although it can be found in stillwaters, carried there by pike fishermen as livebaits for the pike fishing!

One cannot really say that this fish is of interest to anglers. It can form part of a match fishermen's catch, when other species are hard to find but it is a livebait for pike that the gudgeon is sought. The species is tenacious of life and is said to work well as a bait. Tackle to catch the gudgeon can be light and similar to the rig used for bleak fishing. Unlike the bleak, most gudgeon will be taken on the bottom, rarely do they swim in the upper layers of the river or stream. Single maggot on an 18 hook is the ideal bait.

Perch *Perca fluviatilis*

This gaudy, spiny backed fish is found in lakes, rivers and streams throughout the Continent and British Isles. The only country that has a limited perch distribution is Scotland, where the fish is confined to the Lowlands. A member of the Percidae, a group of spiny finned carnivorous predatory fishes, this species provides a major part of the spinning sport appreciated by anglers. The perch is famed as the prime target of small boys armed with cotton line and bent pin rigs.

The perch is a beautiful fish. Its deep body, slightly flattened laterally,

93

has two dorsal fins. The leading fin is spined, the second dorsal has soft rays. Both pelvic and anal fins are bright pink. The dark, olive-green back shades to creamy white on the belly. There are a number of dark vertical bars that seem to become darker as the fish reaches maturity. Perch need to be handled carefully. Apart from the spines of the dorsal fin, the fish has sharp edges to the gillcases which can produce a deep gash on the unwary angler's hand.

Perch do not spawn as a shoal. Small groups of fish, one female to a number of males, will breed over sunken trees and vegetation. The eggs are laid in ribbons that attach to the twigs. This spawning method makes the perch controllable, in the sense that managers of coarse fisheries and reservoirs can provide the perch with its essential spawning habitat. They place bunches of twigs into the water prior to the breeding time for the fish. After spawning, the branches, with the attached spawn, are dragged from the water, cutting down on the number of eggs that would have hatched into further predators.

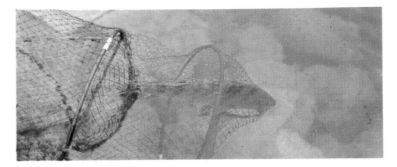

There is little doubt about the feeding habits of this fish. Perch slash into shoals of fry, driving them to the surface. There, we witness the attack as an explosion of tiny fish leaping clear of the water to escape from their tormentors. Large perch become solitary, seeking to attack from the security of a hiding place. Holes, cut under high banks, landing stages and reedbeds all give the shadowed places loved by the big perch. As they get older, the fish cease to chase shoal fish out in the open water and lack of speed necessitates that they strike from ambush. If we read the perch's feeding tactics correctly, it becomes apparent that the angler needs to simulate the activity of its food. Float or leger fishing with worm or maggot baits will succeed because the perch expects to find both forms of food within the .habitat. Livebaiting with minnows is another productive baiting system. Lastly, we have the whole area of spinning or, to put it another way, the presentation of an artificial lure. Perch do not favour muddy waters, nor do they really feed well close to a mud bottom. Without doubt perch are sight feeders. If what we offer as a bait or lure looks inviting the perch will take it

Groundbaiting, when perch fishing, can be useful. The cereal food doesn't pull the perch so much as it attracts shoal fish into the swim. It is then that the perch become interested in the concentration of fish and feeding activity. When fishing on a river known to hold large perch I like

(Left) *Very large perch are not fish that one should restrain in the meshes of a keepnet. They make frantic efforts to escape and in the process the spines on their dorsal fins and gill covers become entangled. This may injure the fish, especially if the mesh gets behind the gill covers. The fish's struggle will also be transmitted through the water to alarm other fish.*

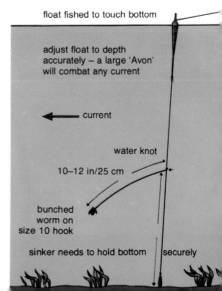

Paternostered worm rig for perch

float fished to touch bottom

adjust float to depth accurately – a large 'Avon' will combat any current

current

water knot

10–12 in/25 cm

bunched worm on size 10 hook

sinker needs to hold bottom securely

to stalk the fish. A paternostered worm, supported on an Avon-style float, can be dropped into each eddy and alongside thick reedbeds where the big fellows are likely to lie. The bait, fixed to move above the bed of the river, is clearly seen by fish. The same method can be used to fish down the stream in steps. A slight lift on the rod tip lets the lead swing along in the current. Lowering the tip gets the weight settled and the bait covering new ground. Exactly the same technique is used to fish a livebait. The bite is not always an obvious dipping of the float. More often you will experience a series of bobbing movements as the perch attempts to grab and swallow the bait. When the float goes down, and stays down, strike firmly. Play it carefully, keeping steady pressure on the fish. Perch have tender mouths from which many an angler's hook has become free and the fish lost.

Perch can be taken on slow-sinking maggot baits intended for rudd and other fish that rise in the water. It is probably the activity of the surface feeders that brings perch onto the feed. Small ones will grab eagerly at most baits, competing with the other species. Older, larger perch are crafty and they need to be approached with the minimum of fuss and disturbance.

Spinning is a great way to seek and catch perch. To watch a good fish follow, then slash at a spinning lure, will make anybody's heart skip a beat. It seems that perch are not too selective in the size of bait that they will attack! I've often had quite small specimens hooked on large artificial lures intended for pike. I think the best lure is a blade spinner. It spins rapidly, creating both a visual and sound signal. If this type of spinner has a shortcoming it is that the rapid spin imparts a severe twist to both reel line and treble hook. The line twist can be removed with a Wye or spiral lead fixed above the trace swivel. The revolving of lure body and treble is more difficult to stop, for the moving treble does not get a clean hold in the jaw of the fish. One feels the strike but doesn't get a securely hooked perch.

Perch also take the bar spoon, especially when the undulating movement shows alternate flashes of red and silver. Probably, the fish's instincts see the spoon as an injured rudd or roach. Keep the spoon down to $1\frac{1}{2}$ in (4 cm) in length, furnished with a size 10–12 treble hook. Perch have fairly small mouths that cannot accept pike-sized hooks!

Resist the desire to keep a number of large perch in a keepnet. Because of their spiny dorsals and spiked gillcases, the fish become entangled, which leads to wounding and distress. There is a shortage of specimen perch in Britain so we must all contribute to ensuring the survival of what we have.

(Above) *Trolling for pike demands silence. The author uses a boat with an electric motor which moves the craft at an ideal speed.* (Right) *This perch grabbed a large Rapala lure intended for pike.* (Below) *Spoons for pike and perch, all with an inbuilt action. The colour variation is considerable.* (Below right) *Blade spinners, sizes 1 to 5. A feather ornamentation has been added to the other two to give attraction while masking the treble hook.*

Pike *Esox lucius*

Far too many anglers reserve their hatred for this fine fish. With the possible exception of the freshwater eel, pike seem to be labelled with the worst of reputations. Certainly they are killers but pike have a function to perform in any fishery. They balance the eco-system, ensuring that there are very few sickly fish breeding a further generation of runts. At the same time the pike is a scavenger, removing dead and dying fish that could become a source of infection.

Only one species of pike is found in European waters although there are another four species within the family. *Esox lucius* is also found in North America, where it is known as the Great Northern Pike. Easily identified, the pike is designed for speed, but speed over short distances for the pike is the supreme predator in most of our waters. The fins are placed toward the rear half of the body to give the initial thrust required by a fish that kills suddenly. The eyes, which seem to follow you as a pike lays on the bank, are facing forward and set on the top of the head. This indicates excellent vision for an opportunist feeder.

Pike spawn in shallow margins in the early spring. The female fish, usually much larger than their mates, are pursued by a number of males that may be less than half their size. The eggs, which stick to water plants, take two weeks to hatch into tiny larval forms that attach themselves by a sticky gland on the head. Although feeding on plankton in their early development, pike fry soon learn to predate upon the lesser animal forms. When mature, pike feed on fish, amphibians and invertebrates. Pike react to angler's baits that represent the shape, smell or movement of the fish's natural prey. Their instinctive urge to kill is often their undoing!

Unlike the perch, which can be fished for with conventional float or leger tackle, the pike has been the subject of much specialized tackle development. Rods are made specifically for pike fishing, along with an armoury of rigs and lures. If we look at fishing with the natural bait, there are two basic methods; livebaiting and deadbaiting.

At one time livebaiting was the principal technique for catching pike.

What fish see depends on the refraction of light through the water. The fish can clearly see the angler in a circle above its head. The bottom is visible in a shaded area round the clear circle because the image is reflected from the surface.

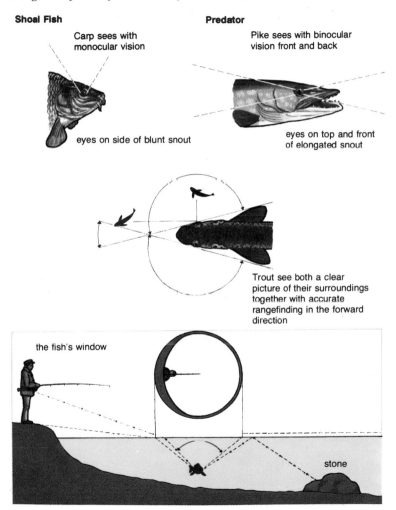

Shoal Fish

Carp sees with monocular vision

eyes on side of blunt snout

Predator

Pike sees with binocular vision front and back

eyes on top and front of elongated snout

Trout see both a clear picture of their surroundings together with accurate rangefinding in the forward direction

the fish's window

stone

The use of livebaiting depends on two factors to be borne in mind:
Shallow water, where the fish can both see well and detect the vibrations that are given off by the livebait.
The moral aspect of using a tethered fish to catch another.
I do not intend to take up an ethical position on livebaiting, as it is a decision that must be made by each individual angler. Undoubtedly, livebaiting is a method that catches a lot of pike. But whether it succeeds in luring the larger specimens is questionable.

I use two rods for pike fishing. Because the species can grow to huge weights, and one never really knows the size of fish on a particular water, two different strengths of rod are demanded. For pike up to 10–15 lb (4.5–7 kg) a rod with a test curve of $1\frac{1}{2}$ lb (0.5 kg) balances with line of 8 lb (3.5 kg) or so. For those occasions when I expect, or know, that larger pike are about, I use a stepped-up carp rod which pulls a curve of $2\frac{1}{4}$ lb (1 kg). This rod is used with line of 12 lb (5.5 kg). Both rods are 10 ft (3 m) in length which give adequate control over casting and fighting fish. Incidentally, both rods have another purpose. The lighter instrument can be used as a spinning rod and the stepped-up version doubles as a float rod for sea angling from the rocks!

To livebait effectively, I have found that the baits must work

Livebait rig for pike fishing

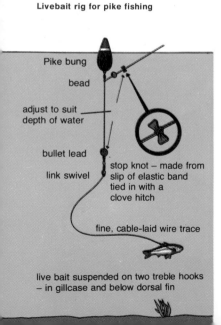

Pike bung

bead

adjust to suit depth of water

bullet lead

link swivel

stop knot – made from slip of elastic band tied in with a clove hitch

fine, cable-laid wire trace

live bait suspended on two treble hooks – in gillcase and below dorsal fin

(Left) *A pike livebait rig. Use a fine-quality cable-laid wire trace, it ensures there is no stiffness to restrict movement of the livebait and that the action of the bait will not kink the wire. The author mounts pike bungs in the reverse fashion to that usually adopted. When put on this way the buoyancy of the float has almost been overcome and a fish will be pulling against a diminished resistance from the bung.* (Right) *Another way to present a small, soft deadbait for pike fishing. Take the cable-laid wire trace through the bait and bring it out as close to the wrist of the tail as possible.*

continually, swimming in a fashion that rouses the interest of pike near to the chosen swim. Over the years I have a fairly accurate record of my pike fishing. Figures show that, regardless of the depth of water, most pike struck at a bait fished well above their heads. About 4 ft (1.2 m) seems to be the depth setting that was most often used. But this isn't surprising if we take a close look at the pike and its eyes. Set on top of the head and facing forward, the pike has binocular vision—ideal for an attack from the depths toward the surface.

The livebait rig uses a streamlined float. I do not like the traditional pike bung, it offers too much resistance to the pull from the pike. They maul the bait, then drop it. I fix two trebles onto a flexible wire trace, setting their position according to the size of the bait, by crimping on with brass ferrules. Flexible wire is infinitely better than single-strand, stiffish wire that will kink as it follows the motions of a lively bait. Try not to put too much energy into casting the baited rig, a gentle swing cast is all that is necessary and it will not dislodge the bait from the tackle.

Deadbaiting involves a legered bait such as a roach, herring or sprat, that is cast out to lie on the bottom awaiting the attentions of a marauding scavenger. The rig differs in that it has to be given a lusty cast to reach deeper water, added to which the pike does have more time to tear at the bait without your knowledge. Using a bobbin to give bite detection will only work if and when the pike moves off with the bait. I have known the bait to be off completely, with no sign of a bite from the bobbin. Because of this, I use a treble hook firmly driven into the bait's gillcase, with a single hook taken right through the wrist of the tail. With

Deadbait rig for pike fishing

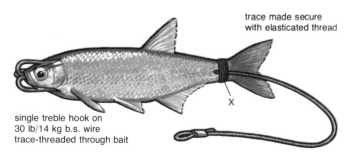

trace made secure
with elasticated thread

single treble hook on
30 lb/14 kg b.s. wire
trace-threaded through bait

X

loop formed with crimp

a soft bait, such as a sea fish that may have spent some time in the deep freeze, I would go further by tying the rig alongside the fish with elasticated thread at point X.

There was a time when pike fishers recommended giving pike a lot of time to mouth the bait before the strike was made. But as the fish sped off with the bait this waiting period resulted in a pike that had swallowed the hook and could not be returned alive. I prefer to strike as soon as I feel a positive movement from the pike. With both rigs, the hook set-up is correct for maximum hooking efficiency.

Spinning is an effective and extremely satisfying way to fish for pike. The advantage over the previously mentioned methods is that one can cover far more potential pike-holding ground. At the same time the spinning art is one of constant movement by the angler. There is no question of becoming bored by watching a float or dough bobbin! All one needs is a 10 ft (3 m) leger rod, which will cope with most situations, a reel loaded to the correct position below the rim and your accessories. These would be a good-sized landing net, a box of spinners and plugs and pliers or forceps for getting the hooks out of a fish's jaw. Forget the gaff—it is likely to damage a fish.

Having decided which lure is right for the day, begin by making a cast at right angles to the bank on which you stand. Retrieve the lure at a steady rate. The next two casts will be to left and right of the first position. Doing this covers the width of the water. Then repeat the exercise but slow down the rate of retrieve; you will then fish the water at greater depth. If the six casts do not produce a strike or a following and interested pike, take a few paces along the bank and start again.

(Left) *There are hundreds of plugs with varied actions. As well as a wiggling movement and the ability to dive, plugs are divided into floating and sinking kinds.* (Below) *The blade spinner (top) can be both seen and felt by fish. The spinning blade sets up turbulence which fish detect as vibrations in the water. Although plugs have an inbuilt action, the angler can make them 'come alive' by altering the speed of retrieval through the water. A sinking plug (centre) can be allowed to sink down, then be returned almost to the surface by a few winds of the reel handle. A bar spoon (bottom) simulates the actions of a wounded or dying fish as it swerves and rolls through the water. An erratic retrieval of the bar spoon will give an action like that of a plug. When pike are feeding, the actions of spoons can be irresistible to them.*

Artificial lure actions

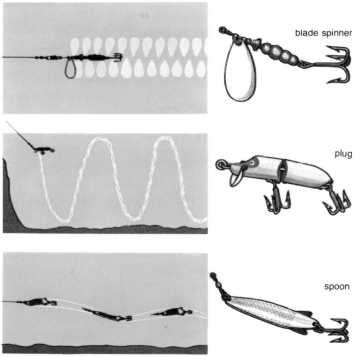

blade spinner

plug

spoon

Progressive movement in this way ensures that your lure will be seen by something—if it is there! It is good fishing technique to alternate the type, colour and action of the lure. Not every manufacturer's spinner will attract fish and pike do have their likes and dislikes that are unaccountable. A lure that gets a response one day can be totally disregarded the next!

Spinners have an amount of in-built motion but most of the work has to be done by the angler, as he varies rate of retrieve or applies side strain to make the lure swerve. With plugs we enter into another realm. Here the manufacturer can build in definite action. He can make the plug a floater or a sinker, a surface-actioned lure or a deep-diving plug that can search out the deepest lake. With these facilities, plus the actions of the thinking angler, the plug becomes a weapon that will enable any fisher to truly hunt the powerful pike.

Pike will follow and take a fly, as many reservoir anglers have learned at the cost of a trout streamer. Where pike are prolific and not of huge size, great sport can be had by presentation of a suitable fly with standard fly fishing rod and line. A short tippet, or leader, of wire or heavy gauge nylon will guard against a pike biting through the fly cast. On a fly rod, playing a pike is a thrilling if prolonged fight. The fish tends to bore down into the deeper water, making powerful surging runs that strip line off at a frightening pace. Steady pressure and a speedy reaction to the fish's movements will bring it slowly to the net.

Fly fishing for pike! This 14 lb (6 kg) pike from Clare Lakes, Ireland, gave Allen Edwards a tremendous fight. It was caught on a fly rod and the fly was tied to represent a small perch.

(Above) *The Fish Lok-a-Tor, an American echo-sounder, gives a picture of the river or lake bed, helping the author to locate pike. It registers fish groups and single large fish.* (Top right) *An out-of-condition pike shortly after spawning.*
(Right) *Support the pike when returning it to water. The fish will swim off when ready.*

The last piking technique that I want to describe is trolling. It consists of towing a lure, which can be a spinner, plug, deadbait or fly, behind a dinghy. On huge lakes, where one often finds huge tracts of bankside reedbeds, trolling enables the angler to cover a lot of water. Rowing is the best method of propulsion; it doesn't scare fish that are lurking within the reed stalks ready to pounce out on a swimming fish—or your trolled lure! Recently, I tried trolling with the boat propelled by an electric outboard motor. Operating with absolute silence and creating practically no wash, I found the motor to be the answer to a pike fisher's prayer. As I was fishing alone, the motor allowed me to give more attention to the rod instead of having to quickly ship oars when trolling under my own power.

I now use one other modern aid to fishing—the echo sounder. The secret of successful fishing is to know what is going on below the surface and to learn what the underwater contours are like. Pike and other freshwater species are not spread like sultanas in a fruit cake! Within their environment they have areas that suit them. Sandbanks, underwater cliffs, deep holes and drop-offs will all offer something, whether it is a feeding place or a secure resting spot. The echo sounder points out these places, and enables us to return to them on other fishing occasions. There is one sounder that is sensitive enough to show not only shoals but individual fish in depths up to 120 ft (36.5 m).

Finally, don't put pike into keepnets unless absolutely necessary. They are easily distressed because very few nets are large enough for the fish to turn round in.

Roach *Rutilus rutilus*

The roach is the angler's most popular fish. It is one species that is found in all types of water, running and still, and in most countries of Europe. Roach provide sport in the warmest summer weather, yet they will bite in our coldest winter. Stillwaters are notorious for going off during the winter months, because they are more affected by the drop in temperature than rivers but even so, roach continue to feed.

There is a lot of colour variation in the roach. Older, larger specimens are nearly black on the back with bold, silver scales along the flanks that shade to a creamy-white underside. The fins are tinged with red, though the anal, pectoral and pelvic fins will be much brighter. Take careful note of the position of the leading edge of the dorsal fin; it should begin directly above the fore edge of the pelvic or ventral fins. If it doesn't, and is placed farther back, the fish is a rudd. Roach have quite small mouths. The upper jaw projects slightly over the lower, which indicates that roach are bottom feeders. The eyes are red and sparkling.

During the months of April to June, roach bear a kind of rash, a

(Right) A roach dorsal fin begins exactly above the front edge of its pelvic fin. A rudd's dorsal begins farther back.
(Below) Two roach trotting rigs. The onion float is for ultra-sensitive fishing; the dart makes casting into wind less difficult.

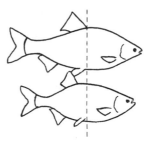

Onion float rig

Dart float rig

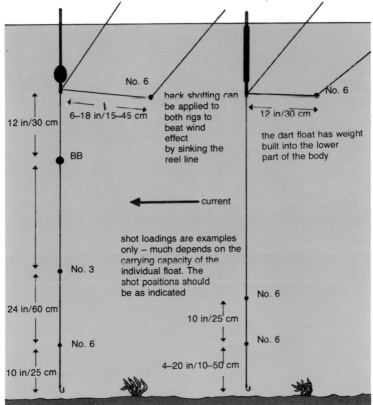

No. 6

back shotting can be applied to both rigs to beat wind effect by sinking the reel line

6–18 in/15–45 cm

12 in/30 cm

BB

No. 6

12 in/30 cm

the dart float has weight built into the lower part of the body

← current

shot loadings are examples only – much depends on the carrying capacity of the individual float. The shot positions should be as indicated

No. 3

24 in/60 cm

No. 6

10 in/25 cm

No. 6

10 in/25 cm

No. 6

4–20 in/10–50 cm

covering of white spots on the head and back. This is a sexual display mechanism that indicates a mature specimen. Male fish are more likely to display spawning tubercles though there can be a pronounced rash on female fish. The male fish arrive on the spawning gravels before their mates and seem to delay their departure till all females depart. There is

The zoomer float rig allows the angler to fish at a distance in running water. The float is loaded, hence the light shotting.

Zoomer float rig

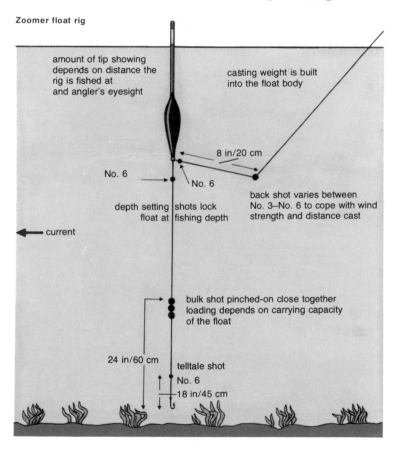

amount of tip showing depends on distance the rig is fished at and angler's eyesight

casting weight is built into the float body

8 in/20 cm

No. 6

No. 6

depth setting shots lock float at fishing depth

back shot varies between No. 3–No. 6 to cope with wind strength and distance cast

current

bulk shot pinched-on close together loading depends on carrying capacity of the float

24 in/60 cm

telltale shot
No. 6
18 in/45 cm

no attempt at parental responsibility, both sexes leave the eggs and larval fry to fend for themselves. Roach are lovers of thick weedbeds, clean gravel bottoms and still to slow-running water. Very few adult fish will be found in the fast flowing stretches of a river. The species can tolerate a degree of pollution, hence roach are found in the dirtiest canal and the muddy, estuarine waters. In warm weather they will swarm into shallows normally associated with the dace. Winter cold drives the roach to seek the deeper water where they compete with bream for available vegetable and animal food.

Roach are shoal fish. They form family groups by size so enabling the angler to hold a shoal within his swim. The fish responds to groundbaiting and constant feeding providing they are not scared by unnecessary noise or bad fishing technique that results in fish being 'pricked' by the hook, then escaping. Their dash through the swim, frightening the shoal, can ruin sport for some time. So hooked fish must be drawn away, after the strike, to be played out in an area at a distance from the feeding shoal. Trotting and stret-pegging succeed as roach-catching methods because the angler covers the river at some distance from his pitch. Care has to be taken in stillwater to get the hooked fish lifted up and away from its feeding companions. Playing a roach unnecessarily will only result in putting the entire shoal off the feed for a long time.

Fishing for this species is a delicate operation. The fish are sensitive to heavy tackle, so the described rigs are much lighter than a standard trotting tackle. The onion float rig fishes well where long casting isn't vital. For extra distance, the dart rig has less wind resistance and the float carries part of its weight loading within the body of the float. Choose floats that carry three or four dust shots as additional sinkers. You will see that both floats are fished single rubber and can be back-shotted to beat the effect of wind. I would use both onion and dart rigs for rivers with a steady flow, canals and stillwaters.

There comes a time when we need to present a bait at long distance but with acute sensitivity. The zoomer fulfils this role in water up to 6 ft (1.5 m) deep. This float casts well because of the weight in the float stem and only requires extra small shots to lock the depth setting and act as a telltale. Bulk shots should be 24 in (60 cm) up from the hook. Try to develop a consistent underhand swing that will flight your tackle through the air smoothly, without the tangles that the more vigorous overhead cast tends to produce.

There must be occasions when, because of adverse winds or casting distance needed, one has to choose legering as the fishing style. In moving water, where there is a good depth of water, a swimfeeder can be

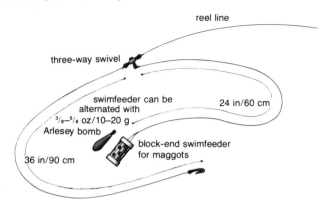

reel line

three-way swivel

swimfeeder can be
alternated with
$^3/_8$—$^5/_8$ oz/10–20 g
Arlesey bomb

24 in/60 cm

block-end swimfeeder
for maggots

36 in/90 cm

a useful addition to the rig. Fish a fairly long trail from the three-way swivel. I like at least 36 in (1 m) with the swimfeeder on a 24 in (60 cm) link. Maggots are the bait. They escape progressively from the block-end, keeping up a steady stream of feed going down-stream past the hookbait. The feed and hookbait can be alternated, using bread to force crumbly groundbait into an open-end feeder with a cube of crust as the hookbait. The main reason for using a feeder on the terminal rig is that you can be certain that the attracting feed is where the hook lies. This style is good for those occasions when roach are known to be lying within trailing bands of streamer weed, only emerging at intervals to snatch particles of food that trundle down over the clean gravel. The feeder can be dispensed with replaced by an Arlesey bomb as the leger weight if you lighten the rig. In shallow streams I leger with the lightest weight available, one that will just hold the bait in position. A single SSG shot or $\frac{1}{4}$ in (6 mm) drilled bullet gives shy roach almost weight-free tackle. Watch for bites on a hanging loop of line between rod tip and water surface or touch leger to a tightish line.

Roach will accept a variety of baits but the larger specimens come to a worthwhile mouthful—the tail of a lobworm is my favourite hookbait for the best fish. All breadbaits are grabbed but the maggot seems to bring the smallest specimens from the shoal. Loose feeding, or better still accurate feeding with a block-end, gets the fish searching and sometimes the activities of the smaller roach create a feeding frenzy that is adopted by the craftier and older fish.

(Left) *A swimfeeder rig designed for roach fishing.*
(Right) *This magnificent catch of excellent roach was shared by two anglers, Allen Edwards and Dennis Burgess, fishing on the River Ansager, near Grinsted, in Jutland. At least six of the fish weighed over 2 lb (1 kg) and all were in prime condition.*
(Below) *An angler swings in a roach from the River Guden, in Denmark. This river has achieved a high reputation for superb fishing among anglers from all over Europe.*

Rudd *Scardinius erythrophthalmus*

This species favours the stillwaters, canals and slower running rivers of the lowlands of Europe. It is distributed throughout the Continent, even into Russia, the British Isles, with the exception of Northern Scotland, and down to the Mediterranean shores. Rudd favour warm waters and will be found in the shallows of most lakes, shoaling in large groups. During the summer months, this fish spends much of the day in the upper layers of water where it feeds on insects. In the cold months, rudd are bottom feeders, exhibiting a liking for the shoots and leaves of the softer waterweeds. They will also root in the bottom debris for larvae and invertebrates.

The rudd is a golden-scaled fish, slightly deeper in the body than its near relative the roach. The fins are bright red and the eyes are orange in hue. Its dorsal fin is positioned behind the fore edge of the pelvic fins.

The species is often confused with the roach, particularly when immature specimens are being compared that lack the depth of colour of fins and scales. Added to this, we find that the rudd becomes involved with the spawning behaviour of other fish that it lives among. There is a great deal of hybridization with roach, both common and silver bream and the miniscule bleak. In fact, the rudd is a sexy little fish that does pose anglers and ichthyologists many problems. Growth, from the fry stage, is said to be very slow although I have seen scales from a 2 lb (1 kg) rudd that indicated the fish was only seven years old! However, this fish came from an extremely fertile lake known for quality fish of at least four other species.

Rudd are a species that can be pulled into the angler's pitch by judicious pre-baiting. I like to carry two forms of feed. A bucket of ground breadcrumb into which has been mixed a mash of soaked bread together with additional, lightly wetted crumb that is needed as a cloud

(Right) *Lilypads and bunched weeds make an ideal rudd spawning area. There are rudd to 2 lb (1 kg) in the lake beyond the channel.* (Below left) *These are Newark needle floats. They come as a kit of four balsa floats matched to engineered, streamlined sinkers which balance the float bodies.* (Below right) *Golden flanks and red eyes – the beautiful rudd.*

bait. The baiting procedure is to get the heavy feed in before setting up the tackle. Spreading a pattern in an arc around the swim means that one can cast to a wider fed area. After a number of fish have been hooked, I introduce the cloud bait. This soft, light mixture sinks slowly down through the water, acting as a visual signal to the rudd. They cannot eat it as it has little substance but the cloud will hold their attention, keeping them within the swim.

After a period of feeding and noting the arrival of the cloud above their heads, the rudd begin to rise up in the water. Then the angler's tactics must change to follow the passage of the shoal. The earlier fishing is done with a light stillwater rig, such as would be used for crucian carp. A sensitive crowquill tackle is dead right. Then as the rudd are seen to turn just under the surface, I alter the rig to bring the bulk shot just under the float ring, filling its position by moving up the No. 3 shot to allow the bait to drop slowly, unhindered by the bottom shots.

An alternative style is to use a self-cocking rig. I admit a preference for this style of rudd fishing. The float is a dart carrying only three very small shots. They are placed one below the float at about 12 in (30 cm) with the second about 12 in (30 cm) back-shotted to beat whatever breeze may be ruffling the surface. The final small shot is positioned some 12 in (30 cm) from the hook to carry the bait down slowly from the top of the water. What happens is that the float hits the water and cocks

immediately, showing a lot of tip. Then the tightened reel line sinks the line and adds the weight of the back shot to the float but the telltale shot does not affect the float until the line to the hook has settled. You get two types of bite: if the float doesn't sink to its correct position make an immediate strike as a fish has taken the bait before all the shots influenced the float's settling position. You can also have the float cocking and shooting sideways as a fish grabs the bait and swims away without feeling any resistance from the lightly weighted dart.

Keep a wary eye open for the lift bite, even though your tackle is set to fish the top layers. Rudd will often take a bait then continue rising to the loose feed you must keep offering to fish that show. The success of rudd fishing is get them into the swim with the right feed and hold them by offering enough loose feed to satisfy the shoal. One doesn't need to tackle up specifically for rudd. A 12 ft (3.6 m) float rod with running line of 2–3 lb (1 kg) is sufficient. The rudd is a beautiful, free-biting sportfish.

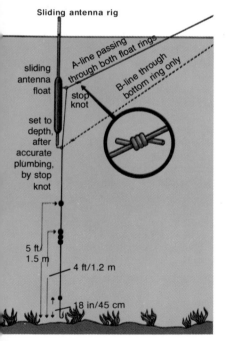

Sliding antenna rig

Not all rudd are taken in shallow waters or in the upper area. This sliding antenna rig can be used in water of any depth. When being fished in stillwaters, the float is attached (A) with the reel line running through both float rings. The method is ideal for windless days when the line lays straight on the surface. Casting over long distances and when the breezes blow needs a sunk-line approach. Then the line is run through the bottom ring only (B). After casting, the float is left as the line is pulled through the float ring by the bulk shots. Do not close the bale arm until the float has settled in an upright position. If you close the bale arm prematurely, the float will be drawn toward you as the shots seek their level, pulling the stop knot down.

Tench *Tinca tinca*

If there is a species other than the tench with a better reputation among anglers for fighting and constancy, I don't know it! The tench is Europe's traditional first quarry of the new season. In June, armies of fishermen plan, scheme and devise techniques that are solely intended to get to grips with this single species.

Tench are found everywhere in the Northern Hemisphere, excepting the Americas and Scotland. Although recognized as a stillwater fish, tench can live and do well in slow-running rivers. The species chooses a water with lots of weed growth and a soft, muddy bottom. This follows from a dietary requirement which is mainly small larval creatures living within the debris that forms the bed of lakes and rivers, especially in the bream zone.

The tench cannot be mistaken for another species. It is a golden-olive colour with the tiniest scales imaginable. The body is very slimy and there was a belief that the tench has medicinal properties. Tench are one freshwater species that do show major external characteristic differences between the sexes. The male fish has pelvic fins that reach back to the fish's vent. In female tench the pelvics are shorter. This species has a barbule sprouting from both corners of the mouth.

Between the months of June-November look for the tench in deep, well-shaded swims. The fish goes into a form of hibernation as soon as the first frosts lower the water temperature. They will emerge from the muddy bottom to feed during bright, warm days of spring in what to English anglers is the close season.

One fishing method stands out from all others when we talk of tench. The lift-float style is both sensitive and heart stopping to use! Its value is that it responds to the feeding habit of the species. Tench grub around in the bed of a lake. Finding a bait, they inspect it, which often disturbs the lie of the offering, causing the float to sway as the tench's huge fins set up turbulence. As the fish lifts the bait in its mouth, any weight that is attached to the cast will also be lifted—and the float will move. What we anglers do is to shot a float to cause it to cock by a tight line between float and bait. A lifted bait causes the float to shoot up in the water and fall flat on the surface.

Obviously, the choice of float and cocking weight must be correct. I like a piece of peacock quill, cut to a size that will cock under the weight of one SSG shot. No painting is necessary, the float is rudimentary but efficient. If the distance that has to be cast is greater than could be gained with one swan shot, I use a larger stick of peacock quill loaded with bulk shots at mid-water that cock it only when the bottom shot is securely on the lake bed. This float doesn't give the same lift effect but at least it jumps up by about 2 in (5 cm) and even I can't miss that.

I know one tench lake that has really deep water close into the available swim. It is at least 14 ft (4 m) deep one rod-length out. Here, the lift method is no good at all, so it's over to another style that I advocate—fishing the slider.

I use a hefty antenna float, capable of carrying at least four swan shot and a BB telltale near to the hook. The float is stopped with a sliding nylon-wisk stop-knot after careful plumbing of the depth. There is no limit to the depth that one can fish apart from what is sensible by float technique. I've fished at a depth of 20 ft (6 m) but that is approaching the limit of the style. Legering must come into play with deep water where I would use a simple rig made up by attaching the lead via a nylon link. This is important if the bottom is composed of soft mud. Any leger, with the weight running on the reel line, would tend to lose sensitivity as the weight would soon sink down into the mud, stopping the free-running

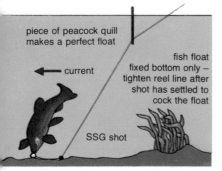

piece of peacock quill makes a perfect float

← current

fish float fixed bottom only – tighten reel line after shot has settled to cock the float

SSG shot

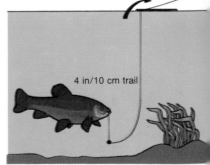

4 in/10 cm trail

of the trace. Bread is my favourite bait with worm a close second. If you choose to use maggot, which I do not particularly like as a bait for this fish, a block-end feeder stuffed with grubs is a useful addition to the rig. At least it ensures that loosefeed is getting somewhere close to the hook.

Tench react to liberal groundbaiting techniques, but not as liberally thrown in as for bream fishing. It must be just enough to overcome the suspicions of the fish. Tench feed well in the half-light and into the dark hours, but bite detection is difficult at these times. So we have to resort to either a lighted float, one that carries a battery to energise a diode, or a luminous one that can be made to stand out from the murk by shining a torch onto its tip. Remember, beware of flashing the beam into the water. Adjust it to shine parallel to the surface so that the light only illuminates what you need to see. Tench soon become educated to the antics of anglers and their lamps. The method I have adopted when legering at night uses a lamp that illuminates both the pitch and a bobbin. The usually ultra-wary tench do not seem to detect danger from a stationary lamp when it is some distance away.

(Below left) *The lift float rig is suitable for water up to three-quarters of the rod's length deep.* (Right) *The author with a tench of 6 lb (2.7 kg)* (Below) *A typical tench water, full of weed and natural food. Due to an average depth of 12 ft (3.5 m), the water avoids excessive changes in water temperature.*

Zander *Stizostedion lucioperca*

This is a species with which anglers in Britain have developed a love-hate relationship over many years. Introduced into the East of England, it has become established in a number of our major rivers and land drains. A predator, it was intended as a culling mechanism for over-populated waters, but has spread widely and become notorious among match fishermen. The species is accused of lowering the quality and quantity of available shoal fish to the detriment of match fishing. That thinking may or may not be correct; but Britain gained another predatory species that will increase our angling possibilities.

Zander were introduced from the Continent, where they are prolific in Northern Europe and Asia. It is regarded as a valuable food species that has the ability of converting quite mundane freshwater fish, with little taste, into exceptionally tasty flesh. In Britain, we are more concerned with the fish's sporting ability. And here the fish scores on a number of counts. It is a good fighter and feeds freely during the hours of daylight and, like the pike, will come readily to both natural bait and spinners. There appears to be little competition between the two predatory species because, given the choice, zander prefer areas of coloured water such as land drains with definite turbidity, whereas pike choose to patrol clear water where their vision is at a premium.

Two fishing methods are paramount. If we agree that zander are fish of autumn and early winter, there being many more interesting species and fishing styles for the warmer months, the angler can choose whether to fish from a stationary situation or to adopt a more mobile attitude to his day's sport. Deadbaiting, with a small roach or dace laid on the bottom of a coloured-water drain, will take zander. The tackle and rig are similar to that used for small pike. An alternative is to fish a paternostered livebait. This style of fishing means that the bait is offered in likely holding places, working upstream. The cast is made by gently swinging the terminal rig out, using a supporting float, to fish for a while

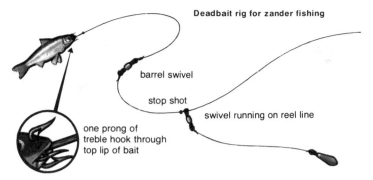

Deadbait rig for zander fishing

barrel swivel

stop shot

swivel running on reel line

one prong of
treble hook through
top lip of bait

in each area. Zander seem to like low light conditions, so the activity associated with a lively bait will have a more powerful drawing effect than a stationary one. It is obvious from the size of a zander's eyes that it can see well in murky water; the fish can easily detect a tethered bait. The difficulty comes in getting them to take our baitfish!

Patience and a fineness of tackle are demanded for the species. Whether acute eyesight gives *lucioperca* an awareness of our lines and terminal rigs is questionable. What is certain, is that the fish is a delicate feeder and the larger the zander the craftier they become. Anglers make the mistake of assuming that a torn bait has been rejected by the zander. What is more likely is that the bait, live or dead, is too big for the fish's mouth. Unlike the voracious pike, zander have a very small mouth which does not allow them to engulf the baits easily. Use the smallest, but liveliest bait that you can catch for this species.

I don't often suggest that a coarse angler should eat his catch. But I'm about to alter that, for here is one fish that does taste good. Perhaps not as tasty as its near relative the North American walleye, but definitely an acquisition for the kitchen and, by all accounts, one that an English Eastern water authority would be glad to cull in quantity.

(Above) *A deadbait rig for zander fishing. Most zander anglers use a nylon trace, but the author prefers fine wire because pike are numerous in fenland drains.* (Right) *The zander is a handsome fish and Continental anglers have a high regard for the fight and the flesh of this battling predator.*

(Right) *The Northern flyfisher's paradise! It is the River Lune at Kirkby Lonsdale, Yorkshire, where the quality of the fish is matched by the beauty of the countryside. The Lune is one of the great salmon and trout rivers of the North of England.* (Below) *A lush growth of waterweed holding great quantities of food and plenty of bankside vegetation typify the river known as a chalkstream, for it flows over chalk strata where rain seeping through ensures plentiful supplies of alkaline water. Trout grow fat but wary in the pure, gin-clear water as they feed on the teeming insect life that abounds.*

THE GAME FISHING ENVIRONMENTS

Rough streams

To many anglers, the most satisfying form of trout fishing is to wander carefree upstream on a tiny beck. Just a cast here and there to likely spots that might hold a bold-coloured trout while savouring the freedom of the moors and boulder-strewn stream as it tumbles seaward. No huge specimens abound in the highlands, the darting trout rarely weigh much more than two or three to the pound or demi-kilo but there is nature to be seen and a challenge to be met in the rough landscape.

Skill is at a premium. The angler must recognize suitable lies, an eddy under the turf bank, where a tiny trout can feel secure. Or the riffle of slower water, downstream of a spray-lashed rock, that provides a respite from the tumbling current. Sometimes the bait is a wet fly, although it could equally well be a tiny worm gathered from a farm midden en route to the fishing. The angler's approach must be careful, each foot carefully placed to gain a foothold on the bed of harsh scree and pebbles. Tackle is light and frugal. Rod in hand and accessories in pocket, the rough stream fisher carries only what is vital to his sport. There is no pleasure in negotiating boulder-strewn shallows and slippery rocks while encumbered by tackle boxes and all the static angler's paraphernalia.

Chalkstreams

In the South of England and Ireland and in parts of Yorkshire lie enormous tracts of rolling chalkland. Rainwater, permeating through the porous rock, collects in underground reservoirs which continuously feed the streams that run off from the low hills. This ensured water supply and the fact that it is highly alkaline spell fertility. All chalkstreams have a luxuriant vegetation and this harbours millions of small creatures. Trout grow large in the clean water, feeding avidly on the multitude of insects and invertebrates that the chalkstream supports. Here, trout can easily grow to very good size if they can escape the predation of man and the natural predators that live in and alongside the river.

Fishing a chalkstream demands stealth. The carelessly thrown shadow or over-confident footfall will soon frighten a feeding trout. Its high speed dash across the shallow river effectively communicates fear to the other inhabitants of the fishery. So, chalkstream fishing is something of an art in approach and then requires no small measure of skill in casting and presentation of the fly. Fly fishing it is, for few riparian owners or fishers would tolerate the use of any bait that wasn't tied in a vice from fur and feather!

Rivers

Game fishing rivers can vary a lot in type and condition. The majestic, snow-fed highland rivers of Scotland and Scandinavia are a typical trout and salmon habitat but both species will also live and breed in rivers where the oxygen levels are miniscule, the pollution massive and competition fierce. Rivers passing through the industrial heart of Britain, for example, still have their run of salmon, although their arrival cannot be predicated with certainty nor is it established that they spawn successfully. Trout are an adaptable species. Pictured always as living in the tumbling stream of clean water, it is sometimes a revelation to find them living well in the turbid, brackish water of a mighty industrial estuary—but they do! Fishing techniques change in big rivers. Spinning, worming and fly fishing can often be practised side by side. Experience gleaned by the regular trout fishers will have suggested and proved a method for their stretch of the river but these men are essentially opportunists. They read their water and make the correct decision necessary to winkle out the fish.

Lakes

Trout in the many lakes and ponds of Western Europe are somewhat at a disadvantage over their river-dwelling relatives. They rarely have a water to themselves, but live in constant competition with a variety of coarse fish species. Known to be cold water orientated, it is surprising that trout are able to tolerate the generally higher temperatures and lower levels of oxygen that one finds in a stillwater. Yet both brown and rainbow trout grow to huge sizes in this habitat. Stillwaters can be extremely fertile, producing great quantities of available protein. It is this factor that allows both coarse and game fish to reach larger weights than would be possible in a river. Trout are also supreme predators that wreak havoc among the young of other species as well as their own. The trout have a difficult time in the cold waters of mountain lakes. There is little vegetation or insect life, so the fish are stunted but, of course, they are still able to reprōduce themselves, further taxing the limited food supply.

In the lowland stillwaters we find a totally different eco-system. Warmer ambient temperatures promote weed growth and encourage the rapid development of the smaller animals. Food is available for all and trout use this food very efficiently.

Reservoirs

Such is the demand for freshwater by humans that there is a constant search for new water resources. Lakes in the high country are dammed to give greater depth, so increasing their cubic capacity. These reservoirs vary little from the lakes that they were formerly, for the larger acreage doesn't cause much of an increase in fish food production. It is by the creation of lowland reservoirs that fisheries of repute are being made. Often, the site chosen is a huge expanse of highly fertile farmland. But these man-made lakes are usually shallow. This factor ensures the lush plantlife that is the foodbase for much of the minute animal life which feeds trout to monumental proportions. When newly filled and stocked, the lowland reservoir produces ideal conditions in which to grow trout. It is almost fish farming in the sense that the habitat is under control. There are few predators until birds introduce the spawn of other fish.

Anglers expect success in reservoir fishing. Fishing costs are high, on the basis that the trout are artificially reared and then stocked at a size which will attract the angler. Put-and-take fisheries are the future of trout fishing; only these waters can now accommodate the mass of anglers new to game fishing. New techniques are continually being evolved to cope with the size of the waters, disturbance caused by wading anglers and wariness displayed by the trout with which the reservoirs are stocked and where they reach huge proportions.

Like all Irish lakes, Lough Beltra holds trout and other species. Unusually, it also provides salmon with spawning redds.

(Right) *A selection of fly rods. Left to right: 8 ft (2.4 m) fibreglass dry fly rod; 9 ft (2.7 m) and 10 ft (3 m) carbonfibre reservoir trout rods; 14 ft (4 m) fibreglass salmon fly rod.* (Below) *Most small, rough streams have their population of tiny highly coloured trout. When the rains come, the spate carries food swept off the high moorlands to the trout as they shelter from the full force of the torrent. Bankside gorse bushes, tangles of shrubs and trees interfere with the back cast and prevent fly fishing, but an upstream worm will tempt the trout.*

GAME FISHING

Game fishing is an uncomplicated sport. There are very few rods employed in fishing for salmon and trout. Reels are simple in construction to perform the function of storing the line yet give adequate control of a fighting fish. Lures are varied, for there are many hundreds of fly patterns, but these can be carried in pocket-sized containers.

Trout and salmon fishing is a mobile sport. Anglers have to cover a lot of water and, apart from lake trout anglers who fish from boats, walk many miles. It follows that tackle must be kept to the minimum; only what is really needed should be carried. A basic shoulder bag with landing net or gaff (for the salmon angler only), completes the game fisher's requirements.

Trout fishing rods fall into a number of types that depend upon the fish being sought and the environment in which they live. Dry fly fishing calls for a stiffish rod that presents a fly accurately and delicately. The length of the rod is determined by the ease of approach to the waterside. Many delightful streams are masked by lush bankside vegetation. Little room is given for casting with a long rod so the angler matches his rod to the conditions in which he fishes. The rod can be made of fibreglass, carbon fibre or split cane. Indeed, this is probably the only form of present day angling where a natural material, such as split cane, still has a useful role.

The dry fly, as the name infers, is fished on the water's surface. The line floats, so can be lifted with less drag and friction than would be expected when fishing below the surface. It is necessary to match the fly line to your rod. Most manufacturers indicate clearly the correct weight of line that a particular rod will handle.

The wet fly fisherman uses a rod with slightly less stiffness. Styles of fishing cover upstream wet fly for small fish on a highland rivulet, to distance-casting on a lowland reservoir. Inevitably, there aren't many rods that would cope with both forms of fishing or the various permutations that fall between these extremes. A standard 8–9 ft (2.5 m) wet fly rod will serve as a useful weapon on most running waters and small lakes. Lake trout fishing from a boat demands that the rod be longer to cope with the strength of potentially larger fish, the need to pick up the line in one action without the numerous false casts that bank anglers are seen to do and give maximum control over fish at close quarters. Boat fishermen do not require the lengthy casting action. Their boat drifts across the lake, broadside to the wind, covering new water and fish progressively.

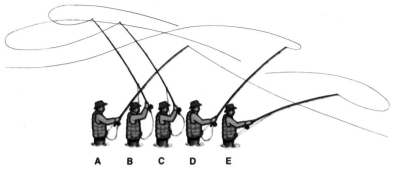

A   B   C   D   E

Fly casting. Beginning with the fly line on the water (A), the rod is lifted smoothly, speeding up just before position B is reached. The rod is held against thumb pressure on the handle at C while the line is felt to pull back against the rod tip. The rod is then pushed forward smartly to position D, which will turn the line in the air, speeding it on the forward cast. The rod tip is lowered to point E, as the maximum line speed is built up. As the fly line flows forward, the gathered line, held in the left hand, is released to shoot through the rings increasing casting distance.

The reservoir angler has emerged as the expert distance caster. Fishing from the bank, or wading to thigh depth, he attempts to cover the water area in front of him at distance and in depth. The rods, developed for this kind of fishing, are generally over 9 ft (2.5 m) long and possess the power to throw heavy lines and retrieve deeply sunk lures used to search out bottom-feeding trout. The rods are abused and subjected to punishing continuous casting. Carbon fibre has become a leading material in the construction of the reservoir angler's rod. It has two useful properties; good strength and lightness. These combine to decrease the weight of the rod and minimize the diameter of the blank, therefore cutting down wind resistance as the angler makes his many false casts whilst extending the line in the air.

When fishing either deep sunk fly or a fly fished just below the surface (known by the loose term 'greased lined fishing'), the salmon angler uses rods that are even more powerful than the reservoir man's tackle. For here the angler is fighting a species that can be of any weight—up to

50 lb (22.5 kg) is not impossible—in conditions of current flow that add an enormous strain to his rod and line.

Much has been written about spinning rods that are suitable for game fishing. In reality, rods used by the coarse fisherman are eminently suitable. Three rods will cover all situations. The first is a 7 ft (2 m) ultra-light spinner for the small stream, especially where undergrowth prevents using a longer rod. My choice for a standard trout spinner is a fast-actioned 8-footer (2.4 m), casting lures from the smallest blade spinner up to a wobbling spoon that could weigh $\frac{1}{2}$ oz (12 g). Used with a fixed-spool reel loaded with 6 lb (2.5 kg) b.s. nylon, this rod will cope with all but the biggest trout, perch and even average-sized pike. My heaviest spinning rod, nominated as a salmon rod, casts up to $1\frac{1}{2}$ oz (42 g) with a small multiplying reel. It doubles as a sea spinner and light bass rod. Two spools are carried, one loaded with 10 lb (4.5 kg) and the other with 15 lb (6.8 kg) nylon.

Salmon anglers swear by the efficiency of the multiplying reel, arguing that it gives better accuracy and playing control over big fish. I definitely find the multiplier more pleasurable to use but there are times when the lowly fixed spool has its uses. Lightweight lures and fishing in

Game spinning rods. Left to right: 10 ft (3 m) salmon spinner, 8 ft (2.4 m) trout spinner and a 6 ft (2 m) ultra-light spinner. All these rods are constructed from hollow fibreglass tubes, or blanks.

extremely poor light call for the fixed-spool where thumb control is not important and over-runs unlikely. Whatever reel is chosen, make certain that it works perfectly, is loaded to the correct level with line and that the drag setting is made before fishing begins.

Fly lines, for both trout and salmon fishing, are manufactured with either of two characteristics; they float or they sink. This function is achieved by building in tiny flotation bubbles along the length of the line, or by having a weighted core to cause the line to sink. Each type of line comes with a defined weight that enables the angler to match it to the casting ability of his rod. Weight, in definite positions, is vital in a fly line. It is the weight along the length of the line that enables it to be cast and therefore carry a comparatively weightless fly out to cover a rising fish.

The water knot

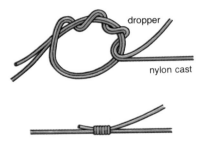

The water knot. This simple knot is used to form droppers on a fly cast. It is made at the time the cast is prepared. A team of droppers can consist of two or more artificial flies. (See page 132.)

There are three main types of fly line. The first has a double taper, in which the line has a swollen centre section, narrowing at both ends to fine tips. The double taper line is the most commonly used and has the advantage that can be turned round on the reel when the leading taper becomes worn. Secondly, greater distance can be achieved by using a forward taper line. As the name suggests, there is a single fine casting taper, swelling out for the bulk of the casting section, that rapidly diminishes to a long, finely tapered trailing section. The forward taper line cannot be reversed to compensate for wear and is slightly more

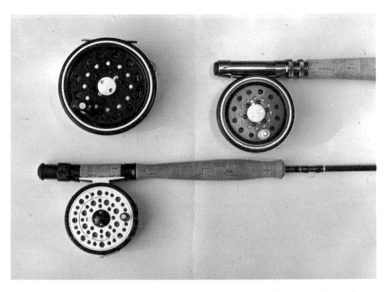

The large salmon fly reel, top right, takes a double-taper line plus 110 yards (100 m) of 20 lb (10 kg) backing. Both trout fly reels take double-taper lines with 55 yards (50 m) of 12 lb (5.5 kg) braided backing. A correct drag setting is vital on fly reels.

difficult to learn to cast with. Reservoir distance casting brought about the need for a third kind of line that had sufficient weight in a short line to cast well. The shooting head was developed, which is rather like half a double taper line backed to a running line of monofilament nylon. The shooting head speeds through the air pulling the nylon through the rod rings with little resistance from line weight or friction.

All fly lines require backing on the reel before the line is wound on. Both double and forward taper lines should have at least 50 yd (45.5 m) of braided Terylene backing spliced to the plastic line. Large trout can easily run off with the whole of the 30 yd (27.5 m) fly line so the angler finds himself playing a fish on the thinner line that is normally next to the spool core. I prefer braided backing, which does not cut into my fingers when controlling a fish on the line. Nylon, moving through the rings at speed, can give a nasty burn if handled carelessly.

We either fish wet or dry for trout. The difference is whether the fly is fished on or below the surface. Wet flies and nymphs simulate an emergent insect or a small fish. There are patterns that attempt an accurate representation of one of nature's creatures. Other artificials, called fancy flies, have been tied subject to the whim or fancy of an angler who had success with his own tying, named it and had it copied by other fly fishers. Far more accuracy is generally found when we consider the dry flies. These tyings are intended to fool a watching trout, lying in the stream and waiting for a natural fly to drift down over its head. The fish has time to inspect the angler's fly and instinctively knows which flies have been drying their wings on the surface. The expert angler will try hard for accurate representation of the hatching natural insect. Presentation—the way in which the fly is cast to alight on the water without splash—is most important. Any movement that seems un-natural will cause the fish to ignore the fly.

There are hundreds of fly patterns, both wet and dry, available to the trout angler. He chooses on a seasonal basis because natural insects hatch at differing times. This means that the angler's choice must match the trout's expectations. Regional patterns emerge, favouring flies of a certain tying, and even trout in adjacent waters vary in their liking for one fly or another.

Dry flies have to be given a little help with a dressing, called a flotant, to keep them waterproof. Although dry flies incorporate stiff hackle fibres, to enable the fly to sit in the surface tension, after a while the weight of the line and hook will cause them to sink. So we apply the dressing, to both fly and nylon cast, at intervals to ensure correct travel of the fly on the water's surface film.

There is another huge family of large trout flies called streamers. These represent fish fry and the larvae of other water creatures. Each

Casting weight can be added to a spinning rig by the addition of rubber twist leads. The line is placed into the slot cut in the lead, then the rubber grips at each end of the weight are twisted to securely trap the line. These leads are speedily changed, for there are no knots to untie. Spinning is a cold-weather sport, these leads save frozen fingers.

year sees more patterns devised to outwit the larger fish that grow in our reservoirs. I have found that the stocked rainbow trout are more inclined to accept the streamer. It could be that these fish, raised in the artificial surroundings of hatchery and growing pond, do not have the experience to learn that the streamer spells danger. Native trout, struggling to survive in the natural lake environment, know all about larvae and insects and feed accordingly!

Artificial fly patterns. 1 Red Spinner, a wet fly based on the olive dun. 2 Black Pennel, a hackled wet fly, used for sea trout fishing. 3 Red Quill, a fully winged dry fly representing the blue-winged olive. 4 Trout streamer flies. Top row, Black Dog, Sweeney Todd (tandem hooks); middle row, Chief Needebah (Matuka), Mrs Simpson, Appetizer. Bottom row, Peter Ross (polystickle) Black Matuka, Black Maria.

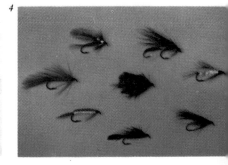

Many anglers fish the nymph to trout in both rivers and stillwaters. These artificials copy the larval stage of the fly's existence. They are fished close to the bottom, where the nymph spends all of its life. If trout are seen to be taking nymphs from just below the surface, the angler reacts by fishing his artificial a little under the surface. This can be achieved by presenting the nymph on a floating line so that only the cast sinks through the top of the water.

Nylon casts can be made up or bought. River fishermen offer a team of three wet flies that are normally presented on a level cast. That means that the strength of nylon is maintained throughout the 9 ft (2.5 m) of the cast. Two droppers (flies behind the point fly), are tied into the cast using water knots, to complete the team of three flies. Nymph fishing can involve using a team of two or more flies but a streamer fly is used as a solitary lure because its considerable weight could cause a tangle in the air if cast with another fly.

Trout and salmon anglers have their own knots although there are times when the coarse fisher's tyings can be useful. All game species are powerful fighters that demand perfect knot tying if the fish are to be landed. Constant casting places severe stress and strain on the lines and knots. Streamlining has shown to be a valuable asset where line

Apart from imitating blue-winged olives and so on, fly tiers produce realistic nymphs like these, the Tiger and Maygold.

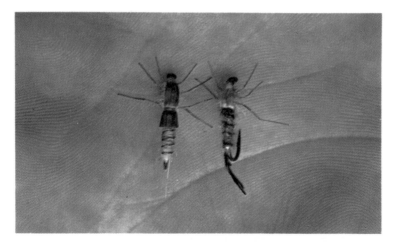

Double turl knot

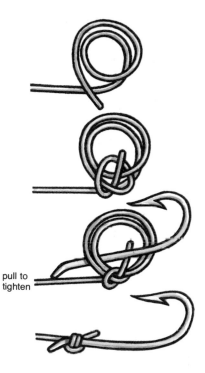

pull to
tighten

*The double turl knot is the last link along the line from angler to
fish, so it must hold. It gives security when fishing with fine casts.*

junctions are concerned. The fly fisher needs to join his fly line to the
cast in such a way as to diminish the possibility of creating turbulence or
drag. The needle knot and whipping knot markedly reduce any friction
as the junction between lines passes through the rod rings and through
the water.

Both trout and salmon can be taken using spinning lures. These can
be metal-blade spinners, bar spoons or revolving Devons made of wood
or plastic. Most of the pike and perch lures will be useful. Brown and
gold, black and blue and silver are colour combinations that attract our
gamefish. The Devon minnow is a bait almost exclusively used by
salmon and trout anglers. The body of the lure revolves as the current

Needle knot

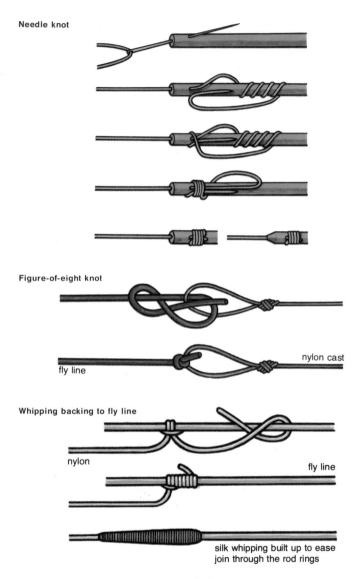

Figure-of-eight knot

nylon cast

fly line

Whipping backing to fly line

nylon

fly line

silk whipping built up to ease
join through the rod rings

(Left) *The needle knot for attaching a semi-permanent nylon leader to a fly line.*
(Centre left) *The fly line can be knotted to a nylon cast using the simple figure-of-eight knot.*
(Bottom left) *Braided or nylon backing should be joined, permanently, to the fly line using this whipped-on knot. The whipping ensures that the knot cannot jam in the rod rings however fast the line is pulled from the reel by the powerful struggle of a fighting fish.*
(Right) *The single turl knot is used for attaching the fly to the cast.* (Below) *A selection of blade spinners suitable for spinning for trout.*

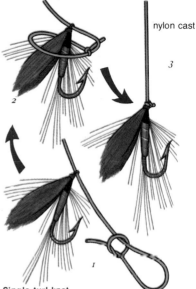

nylon cast

3

2

1

Single turl knot

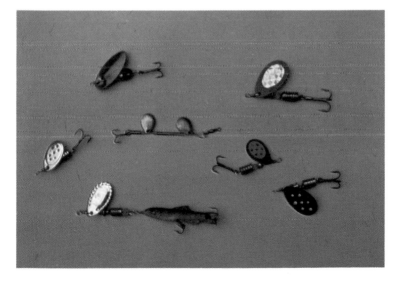

135

strikes the tiny fins angled into it. A treble hook is carried on a separate mount of stiff wire. Wooden Devons have a mid-water buoyancy that keeps them swimming high in the current. To sink the bait in the stream, further weight can be added by wrapping lead wire around the stiff mount. The Devon is a versatile lure that can be adapted to conditions of water flow and the depth at which it swims is easily regulated.

Brown trout *Salmo trutta*

A relative of the salmon, which it resembles, the brown trout is established in most countries of the Northern Hemisphere. Even in the warmer areas surrounding the Mediterranean, this species will be found living and breeding successfully. Man has probably introduced the trout into more habitats than any other species. The exception is the carp, which has an ornamental value in addition to its sporting and food qualities. Many varieties of trout have been described but these are only variations in colour and shape brought about by environmental influence. The sea trout is a brown trout that elects to spend the major part of its life as a marine fish, finding richer feeding in the coastal waters.

Trout inhabit the smallest streams (living in water that hardly covers their backs), the big rivers of Europe where they compete with coarse fish for food, and in most of the great lakes. They were introduced into most of our reservoirs when it was realized that they are a valuable sporting crop that require little, if any, form of animal husbandry. One expects to find the brown trout, like most salmonids, in cold, highly oxygenated water such as would be found in the mountainous parts of Britain. They are there, but also turn up in the most unexpected places. The River Thames has its trout and even polluted rivers, running through industrial zones, will have some fish. The trout can also be found low down the river in estuarine water, where it is given the name slob trout.

Rainbow trout *Salmo gairdneri*

This fish was introduced into British waters from North America in the last century. Originally, the rainbow was intended to be the mainstay of fishfarms producing food, but it was soon realized that the free-rising species was a valuable sporting asset. It has spread to most stillwaters and a number of rivers. The rainbow doesn't seem to remain in a river. Perhaps it reverts to its native American habit of descending to the sea, like our sea trout? Here it is known as the steelhead. Whether the fish

Sea trout   Brown trout

breeds successfully in European stillwaters is suspect. Happily, the commercial hatcheries are able to artificially strip both male and female fish to ensure continuity of our food and rainbow trout fishing!

The rainbow trout appears to thrive in warmer water than would be tolerated by the brown trout. It does not have the same oxygen demand and also has a more varied diet. Rainbows rise easily to an angler's fly and spend a lot of time, when hooked, jumping clear of the water. This species can grow to huge sizes, although many of the big fish reported in the fishing journals were introduced into the fishery after reaching near record weights in the breeding ponds.

Fishing for trout in running water

The decision as to which fly fishing method should be adopted is made for us when we look at the river. If it is of the rough stream variety, wet fly must be the choice. Here a team of three small flies is fished into likely spots either by approaching upstream or as a cast that covers across the river to be swum around in a 90° arc. Presentation is the key to success on the small stream. Nothing, in fishing technique, will replace the knowledge of where trout ought to be.

The tiny fish of the hill or moorland stream take up lies that suit their needs of security, food availability and comfort. Let us consider each of these points and how they affect the fishing. Security means a safe place from larger fish, although these aren't really a menace in small streams because there is rarely enough food for trout to grow large. However, there are avian predators, such as herons, that haunt the shallow waters ever watchful for an easy meal. The trout's food requirement is fulfilled by small worms, washed out from the land mass, the infrequent hatch of water insects and a constant predation on trout of even smaller size. The fish's comfort requires that the adopted lie should not call for too much effort to swim against the current, which at times can be a gushing torrent after heavy rainfall.

So, the trout angler of the rough streams must come to recognize where trout ought to be and then approach his fishing with a lure that will resemble what the little fish are expecting. The flies used by the hill angler are minute. Tied to hooks size 16 down to 20 is not unusual, with a dressing that is extremely sparse when compared with the offerings presented by the reservoir fisher to the same brown trout in lowland waters.

A study in concentration. John Goddard stalks a wary trout with the dry fly. He is fishing the River Kennet, a Berkshire chalkstream.

Walking upstream, to approach the trout from behind with a cast here and there, ensures that the fish do not detect an angler's presence too soon. The cast is made laying the flies out on the tumbling water. Obviously the current will immediately begin to wash the cast back to the angler's feet in a tangle unless contact is kept with the flies. This is done by stripping line back through the rod rings together with a raising of the rod tip. Combined, these actions allow the angler to feel any taps or pulls on his artificials that infer the attention of the trout. It is a good idea to watch the knot, joining cast to fly line, where it enters the water. A sudden straightening of the line should be reacted to by a sharp raising of the rod tip. Long casting is unnecessary because the line and cast of flies cannot be controlled in a rough stream. Try to use a constant casting length that gives both good control on the line when it is fishing and can then be re-cast with the minimum of false casts. Ideally, one wants to lift off the line, make one false cast to measure the next casting position and direction, then lay the line down on the following cast.

Popular fly patterns have emerged over many years of rough stream trouting. The Yorkshire angler's tyings have much to recommend them. Waterhen Bloa, Poult Bloa, Orange Partridge, Black Gnat, Snipe and Purple and March Brown are dressings that will catch trout throughout the brown trout season. Local preference ought to be determined by discussion with successful anglers, although most tackle dealers will stock flies that suit the local waters and demand. Incidentally, these fly patterns are not difficult to tie. Tying one's own box of flies, during the winter months, gives an extension to the sport and a magnificent feeling when a trout is landed on a fly that was 'home made'.

Fly fishing on a river introduces the element of longer casting and bigger fish. The river has a steadier current that swims the team of flies down more evenly. This gives waiting fish a much longer—and clearer—sight of the artificial. Presentation and representation of the natural insect become more important. We try to lay the cast of flies out on the water so that they progress downstream in a natural way. Excessive splashing as the cast hits the surface must be avoided. The angler is now approaching the fish side on, with the flies drifting down to trout. The fish can see what is going on, so the wild cast and consequent poor delivery on the water will frighten fish away from their hunting ground.

The flies used on the larger river make an attempt to simulate a definite aquatic fly. They are tied to larger hooks and the dressing (the amount of fur and feather that makes the body), is greater. Famous patterns emerge, named after the men from angling history who first tied

(Above) *Sheets of polythene foam are ideal for preventing hook points from getting blunted while in the fly box.*

(Below) *The flicknet is attached to the trout angler's belt. It can be opened and ready for action by using just one hand.*

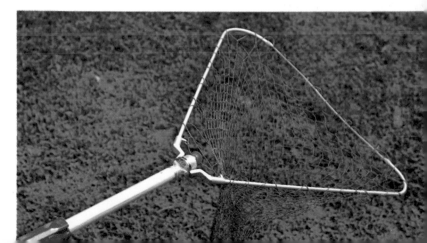

the flies. A feeding fish can often be seen as it rises to the surface to take a drifting morsel. Our flies tend to fish deeper, as the current is slower and there is more time for the flies to get down in the current. Our sense of touch becomes the indication of a striking fish. We feel for the pluck on the line, then react with a sharp raising of the rod. When fishing at short range, the joining knot can still be watched as can the natural bow in the line between rod tip and where the fly line enters the water. The hooked fish can be played out and brought into the net by control on the line. One can play a fish off the reel, particularly if it is a large fish. Correct playing of a trout is achieved by a delicate balance of the spring in the rod and line control as it is slipped through the fingers. Sudden lunges from the hooked fish must be expected and the angler's reaction ought to be immediate. Remember the breaking strain of the nylon cast—it is a fraction of the strength of the fly line! A 4 lb (1.8 kg) level cast for the team of wet flies is about right for both the river and rough stream fishing.

One can buy made-up casts from tackle dealers, or tie them from spooled nylon. The trout angling world uses a system of acknowledged breaking strains that can bemuse the tyro angler. It means that casts are described as having, at the point, an X factor as follows:

$$1X—7 \text{ lb } (3 \text{ kg}) \text{ b.s.}$$
$$2X—5 \text{ lb } (2 \text{ kg}) \text{ b.s.}$$
$$3X—3.5 \text{ lb } (1.2 \text{ kg}) \text{ b.s.}$$
$$4X—2.5 \text{ lb } (1 \text{ kg}) \text{ b.s.}$$
$$5X—1.5 \text{ lb } (0.5 \text{ kg}) \text{ b.s.}$$

The nylon cast is often described as having a taper. This means that a number of pieces of nylon, of progressively lower breaking strains, are joined together. The tapered cast does tend to turn over as the cast is laid on the surface of the water, giving a better presentation of the flies. Its use is more important in dry fly fishing or when a single fly is being fished. Beginners would be better advised to use a level cast, where the same breaking strain is used for the main line and the droppers.

Landing a hooked trout must be an unhurried affair. Play the fish out before making any effort to bring it to your net. When the fish has obviously tired, on the surface and laying on its side, trap the fly line against the rod blank with the index finger. Ease the landing net toward and below the fish, at the same time raising the rod tip to draw the trout over the rim of the net. Then lift the net and carry the fish well away from the water's edge. Trout can jump long after being removed from the water. So recover the fly well back from the water's edge, and where there is a firm foothold. Trout can be killed by a sharp blow on the top of the head, it is both quick and humane.

This catch of four handsome brown trout was made on Lough Dromore in the late evening. Yet another successful evening rise!

Trout fishing in stillwaters

Angling in lakes and reservoirs is totally different from that in rivers, though we use very similar equipment. Stillwaters have no current to work the flies, therefore the action and movement must be imparted by the fisherman himself. The flies are cast to where the fish are thought, or seen, to be feeding. This doesn't mean that prodigious distances have to be achieved for it is in the margins that trout find most of their food. Too much wading and exaggerated casting will often drive fish out from the shallows and make them more difficult to catch. Begin your casting parallel to the lake shore, walking around the perimeter, watching for the telltale splashes and dimpled rings that tell of a feeding trout. Then ask yourself what the trout is feeding on. Sometimes you will be able to see the natural fly emerging on the surface; it then becomes a question of trying to match the natural insect from the contents of the flybox. There will be occasions when the fish are seen to swirl just under the surface, indicating that they are feeding on something that is rising in the water. That something could be the nymph form of the winged insect. We approach either feeding situation with wet fly fishing technique, fishing just under the surface but using a floating line. The weight of the flies will take the cast down in the water. Now the angler has to make them fish well. This is done by stripping line back through the rings by one of two motions. If the fish are thought to be feeding on the nymph the line can be stripped back in an erratic manner, intended to look like the struggles of a nymph as it rises to the surface. Or, the line can be brought back smoothly by drawing the fly line through the rings a couple of feet at a time. A pause between each drawing motion often causes the trout to strike at the fly.

Fishing on a water known to harbour big fish slightly changes the angler's tactics. A single fly is used. The trout streamer was specifically introduced to simulate the fry of freshwater species that live in lakes and reservoirs. Brown trout and rainbows are notorious predators, feeding on small fish that may well be their own young. Hence the tying of patterns that represent both species. A single, big fly is much easier to control on the cast and is certainly easier to work in the water.

With no surface-feeding fish in evidence, a change to midwater fishing is demanded. The fly line is replaced by a sinking variety. This doesn't mean a change of reels. Most manufacturers sell separate spools, so it is a sensible thing to equip oneself with two or more spools. The sinking fly line will take the fly down slowly through the water. A faster sinking version, for fishing the bottom and getting down really fast, is a useful proposition on cold, difficult days when trout are hugging the bottom of the lake.

Casting with any of the three types of fly line is the same. What is different is the way in which the cast begins. A floating fly line can be stripped back, lifted on the back cast and the forward casting action made. A sinking line has to be drawn back *and up* through the water before the lifting motion is made. Trying to haul a heavy, sunken line onto an immediate backcast will severely strain both the angler and the rod! Long distance casting is more easily achieved using a shooting head fly line. The shorter, heavier fly line can be regarded as the weight to shoot both fly and backing line through the air. The casting action isn't pretty to watch, but it's effective.

There are times, particularly in the evening, when a dry fly angling technique can be adopted. Sedge flies skitter about on the surface of the lake and the big trout cruise around feeding on them. The fish can be seen, often with their dorsal fins cutting the surface film. An artificial sedge, dropped onto the water, can be worked back in a series of jerky movements that accurately copy the action of the live insect.

Fishing the dry fly

There are a number of rivers in the British Isles, where dry fly methods are paramount. Known as chalkstreams because of the way in which they derive their water, the fisheries provide brown and rainbow trout fishing that is superb in that the angler can see the trout clearly. It is a true hunting form, where the fisherman stalks his quarry to present a dry fly accurately and drift it down in a lifelike manner. The flies are a work of art, fashioned to be as accurate a representation of the living insect as is humanly possible. Being clear and unpolluted, the chalkstream trout gets a perfect vision of both the fly and the bankside activities of anglers. Fishing is often at a distance, with the angler slightly downstream of the lying fish and trying desperately to avail himself of every vestige of cover that grows on the streamside banks. Because of the accuracy of the fish's vision, an angler must merge into the surrounding trees and not present himself as a clear-cut figure on the fish's horizon.

The fly—only one is used on a finely tapered cast—is presented upstream of a fish that has been detected. The current will carry the fly down, waterproofed to float on the surface, to where the fish lies. The fish is watched intently to see whether it moves to inspect the fly or disregards the offering. Even when the fly has been matched to naturals showing on the water, trout will often ignore it!

There can be a number of reasons for this behaviour. The fly may be dragging across the surface. This can be cured by throwing a line that has a looseness so that it falls on the water with a number of bends along its length. As the fly drifts down it remains tethered from the rod tip. This will cause the fly to swing around in an arc. The longer one can keep it drifting down in a straight line the better. Sometimes a waiting fish is looking for the spent insect, one that has mated and then returns to fall on the water to lay its eggs and then die. This creature is known as a spinner by anglers and on a number of occasions I have witnessed trout feeding on the spinner while ignoring the newly hatched duns, the name given to the creature after it emerges from the nymph case as a winged insect. One can only observe the feeding pattern and attempt to find something in the flybox that will tempt your quarry!

Spinning for trout

There are many waters in which we can practise the art of spinning. I say art because I believe that it can be as difficult to fish a water effectively with the spinner as it is with a fly. There are times, in cold months and on waters where there isn't a hatch of insects on a regular basis, where trout will react strongly to a spinning bait simulating the action of an escaping or wounded fish.

I think that trout are attracted by two things, movement and colour. The artificial bait must have an attractive action, accomplished either by a whirling blade or as a result of an acute bend put into a bar spoon to make it swerve and jiggle in the current. Red seems to be favoured. Used as spots or bars on a spoon, usually gold or silver the flashes of red will give the appearance of fins and flared gills. There is no requirement for special wired traces. The trout's teeth don't cut nylon and one wants to disguise the line and trace as much as possible.

I fish the spinning bait slow and deep in the cold months, only spinning high in the water when there is a positive indication that the trout are moving up to warmer water nearer the surface. There is reason to believe that the spinner is not taken as food as a fly would be. Trout, and other predatory species, take up territorial rights to positions in the river that they guard against other fish. The spinner may represent a threat to that possession of suitable habitat. Any fish that attempts to move onto the lie is vigorously expelled. If we spin a lure across the trout's home it may well assume that yet another fish is attempting to move in. I've crossed the vision of a trout with a bait that has made the fish alert on the first cast and attack on a subsequent cast!

Salmon *Salmo salar*

It is believed that salmon do not feed in freshwater. They live off their body fat waiting to spawn in the higher reaches of our rivers. Why then do they take artificial flies and spinners? Is it a memory reflex? As small fish, salmon feed on insects and other fry before journeying to the rich feeding grounds of the Atlantic Ocean. They spend this marine part of their lives harrying shoals of herring and other species. Back in freshwater, some of that predatory behaviour may remain.

Whatever the reason for salmon's reactions it will grab an angler's lures. These can vary from the smallest fly to metal spoons or even mounted herrings. The lure to use is often dictated by the fishing rules for the river. There are fly-only fisheries and there are other rivers where the fishing methods are varied to suit the season.

In the spring, especially when the water is cold, perhaps still running off from melting snow on the high ground, spinning is the successful style. Slow and deep is the salmon angler's technique. Devon minnows

Devon minnows are made in many colours, with sizes between 1 in (2.5 cm) for trout and sea trout, to 4 in (10 cm) for large salmon.

and bar spoons are cast across the current to sink and fish just above the river bed. The lure is not spun in the accepted sense as there is no attempt by the angler to reel the lure back to the rod to get action in the bait. The current does the work, swinging the bait across the river in an arc. After each cast, the fisher takes a pace downstream covering the whole river in a series of sweeps that should effectively take the bait past any salmon that has chosen to lie while gaining strength to continue its journey to the spawning reeds. Salmon don't take up residence in a particular lie for any length of time, unless that lie is close to the spawning grounds. Fish move into lies continuously, replacing other salmon that have gone upriver. What does happen—and this is important to the salmon fisher—is that fish establish lies that obviously offer them perfect conditions to rest. Year after year, fish will use exactly the same places that we, as the supreme predators, come to recognize.

I spin with my 10 ft (3 m) rod, coupled with a multiplying reel loaded with either 10 (4.5 m) or 15 lb (6.8 m) nylon. The choice of breaking strain is made subject to the size and current strength of the river as well as the known size of fish that, over the years, are expected to run up. Terminal spinning rigs are very simple to construct. A 4 ft (1 m) length of trace nylon is joined between the bait and a ball-bearing swivel. This type of swivel is vital to prevent line twist becoming a problem in the reel line. Constant casting and retrieval, especially with Devon minnows that turn at a fast rate, means millions of trace revolutions in any fishing day.

The two-handed spinning rod gives greater accuracy in casting length and direction than a single-handed rod could do. It also has that degree of control over a fighting fish that is demanded when you hook a salmon in fast water.

There can be a variety of takes from this species. The fish can smash hard at the lure, leaving you in no doubt as to what has happened, or the line will cease to carve through the water. The fish grabs the bait and holds it. A difficult decision is required: has a fish got the lure or is it caught up in the bottom? Either way, I strike to certain that I don't miss an opportunity of a fish. Salmon are thin on the ground and one cannot afford to be uncertain.

When playing a fish, keep the rod high. Use its inherent spring to cushion the power of both fish movement and current flow. Never point the rod tip at the fish. Have the drag adjusted so that a fish that needs to take line will get it! Play the fish out of the streamy water into the slack flowing areas. A fish that spends its time in fast water has an advantage. It breathes more easily when water is rushing past the gills. It also uses the current against the angler without actually expending much energy. A hooked salmon in slack water has to swim to breath, cannot use much current flow against the bend of the rod and is tiring all the time. When the fight slackens to a point where the fish shows and begins to wobble onto its side is the time to get ready with the tailer, which is a wire noose that grips the wrist of the tail. I say tailer because I do not like gaffs and there is always the chance of the fish being a kelt (a spawned fish). The

A happy young man with good cause to be pleased. He caught this fine salmon from scenic Lough Currane, in the west of Co Kerry.

The Silver Doctor, a salmon low-water fly, is a colourful, well-proven example of the fly dresser's skilful, delicate art.

law in Britain demands that we return kelts to the river and one cannot do that if the fish has been impaled on a gaff!

Fly fishing for this proud species is really a specialized form of spinning. Although the fly is cast on a fly line, of either a floating or sinking type, the fly is fished across and round in an arc in exactly the same way as the spinner would be. The choice of line type partially determines at what depth the fly will fish. The depth can be altered by throwing a loose belly of line upstream after the fly has settled on the water. This action is called mending the line. What it does is to give time for the fly to get down in the water before the fly line straightens to the pull of the current. Similarly, the fishing depth can be subtly altered by the position of the rod tip. By keeping the tip high and then lowering it quickly, the fly can be made to flutter momentarily as it escapes from the direct pull of the current on the fly line.

Three main types of salmon fly exist that cover the salmon fishing season. In the spring, anglers use heavily dressed, gaudy flies that are mounted on large hooks. This type of fly has weight to get it down in strong water flow and substance to be seen by spring fish that may need stimulation to attack when lying deep in cold water. Tube flies are also used at this time of year. They are dressed, as hair and feather concoctions, around a plastic or brass tube that slips onto the nylon cast, stopped by a treble hook. Both forms can be given additional weight by wrapping lead wire, in small amounts, around the body tube under its dressing. In warmer weather, salmon tend to move higher in the water and they will rise to strike at a fly that hovers over their heads. At this time the angler changes to greased line tactics, so called because in the days before we had both floating and sinking lines, only a slow-sinking type existed which had to be greased to make it float when that facility was needed. The floating line is used at times of low water, during summer and autumn when there has been sufficient sunshine to raise the water temperature. Salmon low water flies are smaller in size and lightly dressed in appearance.

Watched by Reg Righyni, Brian Harris carefully plays a fighting salmon on Newton Water, a beat of the River Lune, Yorkshire.

Undoubtedly warmer weather makes the salmon increasingly active. There are more signs of fish exchanging lies and chasing smaller fish away from the best holding positions. At this time the salmon will move freely to a low water fly that hangs above their heads. In fact, it is not unusual to have fish rise many feet from the bottom, to slash at a lure just under the riffled surface of the river. This infers tremendously acute eyesight and a desire to keep their lie secure from all incomers, artificial or otherwise.

In certain wind and water conditions it is necessary to wade hip deep. A fly-fisher on the River Tweed at Norham.

THE TRAVELLING ANGLER

Angling is an important part of holiday tourism. Many British families now take a fishing holiday abroad to sample the angling opportunities of countries where freshwater fishing is under less pressure than we are experiencing in Britain. Ireland has emerged as a country, free from hampering legislation, where the quality and quantity of freshwater species is superb. There is no closed coarse season in Ireland.

The best way to get across to the fishing is as a party travelling by sea. There are two shipping companies that operate services with car ferry facilities. B & I lines particularly welcome anglers, with services from Liverpool that allow anglers access to the canals, lakes and rivers of the midlands from the port of Dublin. Fishermen planning an assault on the roach of the River Blackwater or the many species of the Clare Lakes, travel from Pembroke, in Wales, to Cork. Most anglers carry a lot of tackle, with coarse fishermen having more than average, so travel by air has diminished for them.

Denmark is another venue for the coarse fisher. At least two Danish rivers have become household names among our travelling anglers. A shipping company that sets out to look after the bait, offering cool storage facilities, must succeed. D.F.D.S. operate services from Harwich to Ebsjerg in Jutland, which leaves a short drive to the Ansager and Guden rivers. There isn't much coarse fishing done in Denmark, the Danes preferring to fish for salmon and trout, which leaves the quality roach and bream free from rod and line pressure.

I have enjoyed fine fishing from the stillwaters and canal systems of Holland, a country that seems to have more waterways than land! It also has the advantage of providing species that we do not enjoy in Britain. I had four different bream in my keepnet recently: bronze, silver, zope and schnieder together with fish that I couldn't immediately recognize!

Anglers travelling by car can cross to Holland from Felixstowe or Dover, using Townsend Thoreson who land at Zeebrugge, in Belgium, from where it is a short ride to the fishing of the southern deltas with only a four-hour journey to the canals and lakes of the north.

Bait is expensive (most maggots are imported from Britain anyway), so take enough for the holiday. I carry grub baits in a cooler box, fitted with freezer packs to lower the temperature. I have found that hotels will store maggots providing they are in such a container. The same can be said of the shipping lines but it is vital that the container has secure fasteners. There must never be any escapees to spoil the good relationship between carriers and the fishermen of Britain.

GLOSSARY

Antenna A float that cocks with its bulk below the surface. The fine tip is little affected by high winds.

Anti-kink A spinning lead designed to prevent line twist.

Back shot Shot attached between the float and rod tip to sink the line in windy fishing conditions.

Bag The angler's total catch.

Baiting needle A long needle used for threading a trace through a deadbait for mounting as a bait.

Bale arm The revolving arm that winds line back on to the spool of a fixed-spool reel.

Barb The sharp, notched part of a hook that prevents a fish freeing itself. Barbless hooks are becoming popular among sportfishermen.

Bite An indication to the angler, by sight, sound or touch, that a fish has taken or mouthed the bait.

Blank A solid or hollow fibreglass length from which rods are made.

Bomb A casting lead of any size shaped like a bomb, with a swivel on the small end.

Bread flake Bread from the soft inside of a new loaf.

Breaking strain (b.s.) The test pull on fishing line measured in pounds or kilogrammes when it breaks in the dry state.

Bung A large-bodied float.

Butt indicator A bite indicator used near the butt-end for legering.

Caster Chrysalis stage of a maggot.

Casting Throwing line out by using the flexibility of the rod.

Centrepin reel A reel with the spool releasing line parallel to the rod.

Closed-face reel A fixed-spool reel with the line issuing from a hole in a

cap covering the face.

Cloud bait Fine groundbait which sinks in a cloud and triggers off feeding activity in fish.

Controller A weighted float used for casting very slow-sinking, light baits.

Dapping Presenting a bait without casting, usually from between bankside vegetation.

Deadbaiting Fishing with dead fish for predatory species.

Devon A lure that spins round a wire mounted with a treble hook.

Drag Unnatural movement of line on the water. A slipping clutch on fixed-spool and multiplying reels.

Drain Man-made waterway draining low-lying and fenland areas.

Dropper A hook link of nylon or wire attached to the main line.

Drum A spool round which the fishing line is wound.

Fixed-spool reel A reel which has the spool at right angles to the rod. A revolving arm picks line up and winds it round the spool.

Float fishing Using a float to register bites from taking fish.

Fold-over lead Flat lead that can be folded over line to add weight.

Freelining Fishing a bait without float or weight.

Gaff Pole mounted with a hook to lift heavy fish from the water.

Groundbaiting Feed thrown into a swim to attract and hold fish.

Hook length Nylon of varying lengths carrying a whipped-on hook and a loop at the other end for attaching to the reel line.

Keepnet A tube of netting sealed at one end to keep the angler's fish alive.

Laying-on Float-fishing with the

bait weighted to stay on the bottom.

Lead Weight used to cock floats or as leger sinkers.

Legering Fishing without a float and with a sinker to hold the bait on the bottom.

Line bite Misleading movements of the line as fish accidentally brush against it.

Link swivel Quick attachment device for traces and casts.

Loaded float A weighted float.

Lock shot Split shot placed either side of the float ring to fix its position and bait depth.

Lure Any artificial bait.

Maggot dropper A tube filled with maggots and lowered into the swim to open and release them in the area of the baited hook.

Multiplying reel A centrepin reel with a gearing to turn the spool three or more times with a single turn of the handle.

Nymph A larva of the Ephemeridae family of flies, or an angler's artificial representation.

Over-run Bunch of confused line on the spool of a multiplier or centrepin caused by inefficient casting.

Paste Stiff bread dough used as a hookbait.

Paternoster Terminal tackle with the lead at the bottom and the hooks above on booms.

Peg A numbered fishing position.

Pennel tackle A rig with two hooks mounted in tandem.

Pitch Angler's fishing position.

Plumbing Finding the depth of the water by using a plumb bob.

Quivertip A rod-tip bite indicator.

Rings Circular guides fixed to rods that spread the stress along its length while playing a fish or during casting.

Pole A long, many-sectioned rod. The line, of fixed length, is attached to the rod-tip.

Rod rest A stand upon which rods can rest during legering.

Shot load The amount of lead a float will carry before sinking.

Slider A float held by a stop-knot to allow fishing at a depth deeper than the length of the rod.

Specimen A fish heavy in relation to the average weight of the species.

Split cane Cane lengths glued to form the sections of a rod.

Springtip A form of quivertip (which see) but with a spring to indicate bites.

Stret-pegging Float fishing down a river in stages.

Strike The sharp movement of the rod to set the hook home.

Swim An area known to hold fish.

Swim-feeder Container attached to terminal tackle to allow feed to trickle out and attract fish.

Swingtip An arm attached to the rod tip which indicates bites when moved by taking fish.

Taper The amount of decrease in diameter of a rod from butt to tip.

Terminal tackle The rig or trace ending with the baited hook.

Test curve The pull on line that brings it into a right angle with the rod. Used to determine the balanced b.s. for the rod.

Trace Length of nylon or wire used to form a rig or terminal tackle.

Trotting Allowing the current to carry the float and bait away downstream while retaining touch on the line. Best accomplished with a centrepin reel.

Zoomer An antenna-type float with built-in weight.

INDEX

Page numbers in **bold** refer to main
entries.
Page numbers in *italics* refer to
illustrations.

Acknowledgements

Dr Dietrich Burkel for the illustrations of our freshwater fishes.

Chris Jones for his tackle drawings.

Trevor King, of Dubery's Fishing Tackle, Hornchurch, Essex, for the loan of tackle and odds and ends that I couldn't find in the box.

Mustad, for use of the illustration of hooks on page 29.

Lowrance for their help with echo sounders and fish finders.

Mrs. Debbie Prichard for her work on the manuscript.

Fishing companions, far and near, for their help and patience with me over many happy years.

Len Cacutt for copy editing and advice

Caroline Hill—art editor and cover designer

Goodwin Dorman—design

Robin L. K. Wood—editor